# Praise For <u>the</u> Guide

\*\*\*

Tested at the South Bay Jewish Community Center, Torrance, CA; also at THE UNIVERSITY OF JUDAISM in Los Angeles, where 70 attendees rated the experience "wonderful" and "excellent ."

\*\*\*

"Here is one more tool for women to understand their own culture and background and reach greater empowerment. Consciousness-raising provides a think-tank for women—a chance to listen and learn from each other. *The Jewish Women's Awareness Guide* is a wonderful new vehicle!"

—*Diane Welsh, President, NOW-NYC*

\*\*\*

"...I am impressed with the way the opening exercise questions are framed...reading them made me want to relax and talk."

—*BRIDGES Magazine, Seattle, WA*

\*\*\*

"...in this new book, three feminists argue that 'the group' is the essential unit in which a Jewish woman can find herself...the book suggests how to put a group together and the kind of thought-provoking questions with which it might engage..."

—*THE JEWISH JOURNAL, Los Angeles*

\*\*\*

"Congratulations and thanks on the publication of the *AWARENESS GUIDE*...a most useful volume, beautifully produced...should prove invaluable to the ever-growing number of Jewish women who are defining themselves as feminists, neo-feminists or veterans."

—*ISRAEL WOMEN'S NETWORK, Jerusalem*

\*\*\*

# THE JEWISH WOMEN'S
# AWARENESS
# GUIDE

BIBLIO PRESS
NEW YORK

In memory of our mothers

Leah Schmukler
Sara Kroopnick
Helen Yankelowitz

For our daughters and sons

Erica and Jill
Joshua, Ilana and Shoshana
Linda, Randi, Judith, Edward and Steven
and
in loving memory of
Larry Carnay

and thanks to

Steven J. Weinberg & Rabbi Sheila P. Weinberg
&
Dorna Silverman

**2nd printing 1993**

© *Biblio Press, NY.*
*All Rights Reserved. No part of this publication may be reproduced by any means,*
*electronic or print, in whole or in part, without permission. For information, address Biblio*
*Press, 1140 Broadway, New York, NY 10001.*

*Library of Congress Cataloging-in-Publication Data*

*The Jewish women's awareness guide : connections for the 2nd wave of*
*Jewish feminism / by the "New Woman" Collective; Janet Carnay . . .*
*[et al.].*
     *p.   cm.*
*Includes bibliographical references.*
*ISBN 0-930395-14-X : $7.95*
     *1. Women, Jewish—United States.   2. Feminism—United States.*
*3. Women in Judaism—United States.   I. Carnay, Janet.   II. New*
*Woman" Collective.*
*HQ1172.J486   1992*
*305.48'696—dc20*                                          *92-2894*
                                                             *CIP*
Cover quotation from
*Betty Friedan: Fighter for Women's Rights,* Sondra Henry and Emily Taitz,
Enslow Publishers, Hillside, NJ, 1990.

# THE JEWISH WOMEN'S
# AWARENESS
# GUIDE

\* \* \* \* \*

### Connections for the 2nd Wave of Jewish Feminism

by

## THE "NEW WOMAN" COLLECTIVE

### Janet Carnay    Ruth Magder    Laura Wine Paster
### Marcia Cohn Spiegel    Abigail Weinberg

BIBLIO PRESS
NEW YORK

# THE JEWISH WOMEN'S AWARENESS GUIDE

## CONTENTS

# STARTING NOW AND LOOKING BACK*

*The recent past is more difficult to define than decades of history. Standing on the shore of the present, the incoming tide spills toward us in divided directions, while the distant waves appear precise in their parade forward.*

*Thus, many view the American women's movement as now being in a third stage, with the first starting in the mid-19th century[1] ending in the 1920s when the women's vote was won,[2] with a hiatus that closed in the early 1960's with the Friedan influence and the formation of the National Organization of Women (NOW) in 1966 as a second stage. A third stage is seen as the present 90's, a post-modern period when emancipatory gains during the past thirty years in personal, economic and political spheres is experiencing a struggle for retention and expansion.*

*Jewish women's awareness has a different time-frame, especially in view of the critical mass of Jewish population[3] before W.W. I and again in the 20's to the 40's into the post-Holocaust period. While we know of Jewish women adherents in American suffrage and social reform efforts, their names appear as trade union, social service, Jewish education and philanthropy movers. When we think of "Jewish feminism", we refer to the early 70's (eight years after the publication of **The Feminine Mystique** by Betty Friedan), when Ezrat Nashim, the first Jewish offshoot group began, now marking the first stage of Jewish women's awareness of a Jewish agenda. 1973 itself is now seen as the opening of a broad call for Jewish women's rights. While Reform women achieved the rabbinate in 1972, it is that time until 1985, when women won the right to become Conservative rabbis, that a foundation was in place to consolidate gains in the secular and religious spheres. Thus, for the purpose of this Guide, we have chosen to consider 1970–90 as a "first stage," and the present period in the 90's, as a "second stage."[4]*

*This Guide addresses itself to Jewish women of all ages and groups. Of special value to readers, is the following account of the FNJWC—the*

**\*Text by Ruth Magder; italicized content by Doris B. Gold.**

*First National Jewish Women's Conference of 1973, as seen by Ruth Magder of the "New Woman" Collective.[5] As a recent college graduate, she is summarizing that event, in the context of her student experience in a Jewish group:*

Here we were, gathered to discuss in 1989, the founding of a Jewish feminist group at our college. Before us were straight women, lesbians, Orthodox women and others who were unaffiliated; some with little formal Jewish education, sitting with some who had graduated from yeshiva high schools. Each of us had her own vision; common to us was the need to create a place for us to meet, discuss and define our identity as Jewish women.

(Later, I decided to submit my Senior thesis on this experience. I read whatever I could find to shed light on the subject in conference reports, articles and books, especially on the 1973 Conference and what Jewish women had achieved since the onset of the women's movement itself. I interviewed ten Jewish women who had been active at that time and later on.)[6]

These are some of my thoughts about that event:

The late 1960's held great promise for Jewish women. The women's movement had heightened awareness of women's lives and caused many to re-examine their views. During the 1967 Arab-Israeli war, increased interest in ethnicity arose in the US, fostering a renewed sense of Jewish pride. But despite the two trends, each flourished independently of the other. The voices of Jewish women were conspicuously absent from the women's movement. Despite what seemed like many Jewish women participants, few spoke as Jewish women. It seemed as if the women's movement did not have a place for Jewish women to be Jewish. Some went so far as to deny their Judaism. Even women with strong Jewish identities failed to connect their Jewish and feminist concerns.

The Jewish community barely recognized the changing status of women. The modern Orthodox and Conservative movements continued to deny women access to ritual leadership roles. Reconstructionist and Reform groups granted more options, including rabbinic ordination, but theological equality did not cancel bias against women, so ingrained were communal practices. Jewish tradition celebrated the domestic role of Jewish women, avoiding their involvement in critical problems, with severe under-representation in leadership positions, and undervaluing women's work as volunteers. The negative stereotypes of domineering, materialistic Jewish women prevailed.

Over time, the women's movement developed more particularity, with women identifying themselves as Black, lesbian or disabled, etc., and soon some Jewish women insisted that they themselves be included as Jewishly identified. Grass-roots discussion groups arose to raise consciousness (CR), which encouraged women to examine their own personal development and define their grievances. For some, this also meant an exploration of their Jewishness. Women, whose commitment to Judaism included the struggle to maintain a balance between secular norms and Jewish values, began to apply feminist analyses to the status of women in Jewish life.

One of the earliest and most vocal critiques came from a group of women called "Ezrat Nashim"—literally, "the aid of women," also a women's gallery of a traditional synagogue of the same name. The group was begun in 1970 when female members of the New York Havurah realized the need to educate themselves about the status of women in Judaism. (The havurah, like others of its kind, was a Jewish prayer community.) The disparity between strong ideological commitment to egalitarian worship and actual discriminatory practices in that movement fanned women's frustrations, and by 1971, Ezrat Nashim broadened its scope to include political action. Group members began to speak publicly in many forums in the US, borrowing from the student tactics of the 60's with sit-ins and calls for the desegregation of synagogue life and Jewish ritual. Their activities called attention to their grievances as Jewish women. However, this discontent was not limited to religious circles—also dissatisfied were women in the Jewish radical left and women in the Jewish establishment. However, those women were isolated.

By 1972, efforts were begun to bring Jewish women together. Jewish women students formed caucuses to communicate common issues. The strongest Jewish student organization of the 70's and 80's was Network. In its attempt to attract credibility for critical issues, it seized upon Jewish women's discontent, and under the guidance of Sheryl Baron and Vivan Silver-Salowitz, the First National Jewish Women's Conference was planned—a radical undertaking, unprecedented in scope.

This ambitious event was held Friday, Feb. 16, 1973 through Monday, Feb. 19, in NYC with some 500 women attending 33 separate forums. The speakers included Orthodox women, radical Zionists, Congresswomen, writers, educators, rabbinical students and Jewish professionals. Even a session on prostitution and another on volunteerism in the Jewish community was scheduled. There was a multi-media show and prayer services that were conducted by women. Workshops, large-panel presentations and small group discussions were included. To secure financing for this event, the coordinators secured limited funds through Hillels and other campus groups, as well as the Women's Division of the

3

American Jewish Congress and the NCJW. (Natl Council of Jewish Women). Disproportionately, the participants were from the NYC metropolitan area, but some women came from other cities and Canada. Many expectations emerged but could not be fulfilled at this outpouring, nor did the FNJWC address a broad range of feminist issues. Complaints arose about the cost of the conference which seemed to prohibit participation by a cross-section of women. For most attending the event, there was an assumption of affiliation with organized Jewish life, an assumption not shared by all.

And inevitably, a religious conflict arose between the women in Ezrat Nashim and a group of Orthodox women, when the former group planned "traditional" prayers. It was felt that having a prayer service led by and for women was an act of equality, but the others saw this as a violation of Orthodox custom. Other ritual questions arose, and in the end each woman who attended a Shabbat morning service made her own decision concerning minyan rules, etc.

Later, a protest by a group of Jewish lesbian women occurred on Saturday afternoon's panel, in "Growing Up Jewish." It was then that those woman demanded an opportunity to be included. They were angry because of the lack of inclusion of a lesbian speaker and the fact that none of the sessions addressed homophobia or gay/lesbian rights. They too repeated the protest over the cost of the event which seemed to shut out poor women. (Later a workshop on "Growing Up Gay" was added to the agenda, which attracted over a hundred women of all sexual orientations—an indication of the important role lesbians and bisexuals would come to play in the future of Jewish feminism.)

Finally, the FNJWC was not felt to be a groundbreaking event to radical feminists, and traditional women did not consider their agendas addressed. The event failed to change or enrich the ideas of those few women already active as Jewish feminists. Some projects were begun as the result of the conference, but unfortunately most, with the notable exception of LILITH Magazine, did not endure.

However, despite its shortcomings, the FNJWC was a landmark. Even its disruptions provided an education to Jewish women—alternative ideas to the narrow confines of women's roles as had been defined in the early 1970's. At this event, which included only one session where men attended, women's leadership was visible, showing the potential of a Jewish women's agenda. This positive visceral response surely helped pave the way for a movement toward religious reform regarding the status of Jewish women. The occasion provided a first experience of networking with others, especially sharing common frustrations and "sisterhood" in a new dimension.

4

At the same time that this kind of Judaism experienced a resurgence, few instruments for Jewish women's expression existed. In the American women's movement, Jewish women found it hard to address their Jewish concerns. In Jewish groups, cultural and religious customs limited the opportunities for action. Not wanting to abandon either side of their identity, Jewish women were without an energizing force. The Conference did finally provide a welcome third alternative to this dilemma, with Jewish women's groups eventually focusing on issues that attracted their interest.

Since 1973, numerous changes have occurred in the status of Jewish women. The "denominations" have responded with greater or lesser force to calls to broaden the spiritual and ritual options of women, and to grant women a wider role in religious life. Presently, women comprise about half the rabbinic students at the Reform Hebrew Union College. The outpouring of information about Jewish women's status is large and still growing, with universities and other bodies heeding the call to make Jewish women more visible to themselves. Without providing a complete balance sheet of Jewish women's accomplishments since 1973, it is surely clear that more recognition, in synagogues, in halacha governing Orthodox women, and in the Jewish intellectual and university sphere, and in leadership roles, are still lagging.

While there is now discourse on aspects of Jewish women's lives, many women have not yet formulated their stance on either "personal" or "political" items. Having speakers on Jewish women topics provide "fundamentals" only, as being "in vogue," but often it is considered inappropriate to raise important women's issues. On many levels isolation persists, and especially unforged are the links to the American women's movement when issues of justice could and should have Jewish input, especially concerning civil and social rights, and where actions about Israel and anti-semitism still arise.

The need to challenge the isolation and alienation of Jewish women continues. In 1973 the Network women attempted to confront this condition. In 1989, the young women who met at my college attempted to fill this need once more by forming a group to validate our experiences and visions of Jewish life. Throughout history, Jewish women's ties to each other have been strong. Now once more we hope to stimulate women to come together. The knowledge of self, combined with the support of like-minded people, gives us the opportunity to define issues as we see them—knowledge which might lead to action.

*In the face of the complexity and diversity of issues that concern us Jewish women, we think the Guide which follows can help us confront ourselves to reach a high level of understanding. We have drawn on the* experiences of five different women on both the East and West coasts and their knowledge of Jewish feminism. It is our hope that the value of this Guide will further the process that began almost twenty years ago, and that we shall be renewed by it. And, paraphrasing one part of our own Passover Hagadah, we think it is incumbent on every Jewish woman in each generation to look upon herself as if she had actually experienced her own people's history, as it is said, and to bring herself to her place of understanding of equality, in Israel and in America. . . . Amen!

(1) Women's Rights Convention, 1848.
(2) That period also produced changes in Jewish women's awareness. Jewish women demanded mixed seating in synagogues.
(3) The exodus from Eastern Europe between 1880–1910. Jews from Germany and Poland (150,000) came to the USA between 1860–70, but between 1880 and 1945, the country gained 6 million Jews.
(4) However, Judith Plaskow, the theologian, in *Standing Again At Sinai,* (1990), speaks of the present period as a third stage for Jewish women.
(5) See back cover for brief biographies of each woman in the "New Woman" collective.
(6) Women interviewed were: Sheryl Baron, Shifra Bronznick, Aviva Cantor, Eva Fogelman, Judith Hauptman, Paula Hyman, Jacqueline Levine, Isabella Meltz, Judith Plaskow and Judy Segal.

# PREFACE

Three of us came together through our connection to the Jewish community. In 1977, Janet and Laura met when their families joined a Havurah through their synagogue. Laura and Marty (Marcia Cohn Spiegel) met in 1980 as a result of the Conference on Alternatives in Jewish Education. Janet and Marty met at a conference on Jewish women's creativity in 1986. The following year the three of us worked together for the first time to plan a woman's retreat, "Transforming the Ordinary," under the leadership of Myra Diamond and the auspices of the Jewish Federation Council of Greater Los Angeles.

We were drawn together by our common interest in women's creativity and spirituality, our concerns for Jewish family life, our desire to build community among women, and our dedication to encouraging women to find their true voice and risk change. We found that these common interests were based on our ongoing examination of our own lives and our drive to use our experiences, the struggles and the pain, to help other women understand their lives. This drive is the source of much of what we do, personally and professionally, both together and as individuals.

In the spring of 1991, Doris Gold and Biblio Press had already started working with Ruth Magder and Abigail Weinberg in New York City to plan the *Awareness Guide*. Ruth and Abby, women in their 20's, had been involved with other college women exploring Jewish identity. Doris invited us to collaborate on this project, so the five of us became a cross-country "collective". The three of us in California saw this as an oportunity to reach out to women beyond our immediate community and to put into writing the ideas we had been exploring, discussing and teaching for many years. Appropriately, nine months later we all wrote the final words.

During the nine months of our working together, it became clear that what we had produced as a team was greater than what any one of us could have done alone. We had brought to this task our individual skills and talents and created a collective voice that spoke for us all. We learned some new and essential skills: to be still and truly listen to each other; to leave our egos outside of the writing space; not to be attached to the

7

rightness or wrongness of our ideas or to our own words; to feel free to express ideas that might not work, without fear of failure or judgment. Integral to the process was laughter, which enabled us to dissipate the intensity of the feelings evoked by the material and to let the little girls within us play.

Writing *The Guide* taught us new things about ourselves and each other. As we answered every question that we wrote, we saw pieces of our lives of which we had not been aware. Because we recognized that our responses reflected only our own life histories, we invited other women into the room through our imaginations: first our own sisters, then women we knew, and then, women we didn't know, whose life styles and experiences were different from our own. The women unbeknownst to them, who helped us to write this *Guide* include: Rosh Hodesh Alef and Rosh Hodesh Bet (South Bay, Los Angeles), the women of B'not Esh, the Los Angeles Chai Chapter of Na'Amat, the sisterhoods of Temple Beth El (San Pedro, CA), Temple Menorah (Redondo Beach, CA) and Congregation Ner Tamid (Rancho Palos Verdes, CA), the Mikvah Ladies, Shabbat Shenit, Debbie Friedman, Olivia Schwartz, Barbara Waxman, and Ursula Sherman. And we expecially want to thank the Thursday Night Group of the South Bay Jewish Community Center who were the first to try this material and showed us some of its possibilities and its limitations.

We have tried to frame the questions to include Jewish women of every age, educational background, working status, economic class, ethnic background, sexual preference, marital status, family constellation, physical ability, religious practice and belief, and women of all degrees of identification with feminism, and all levels of involvement in volunteer service, community organization, and political activism. While we tried to include everyone, there are questions that, by their very nature, will exclude some people. We hope that if this happens, you will be able to use that time to hear the stories of other women and how they resonate with your own.

Though this *Guide* was written from our experiences, there were certain books and publications we kept close at hand for reference. They were: **The New Our Bodies, Ourselves,** by The Boston Women's Health Book Collective; **NOW Guidelines for Feminist Consciousness Raising** by the National Organization for Women; **Deborah, Golda and Me, Being Female and Jewish in America** by Letty Cottin Pogrebin; **Women's Ways of Knowing** by Mary Field Belanky, et al; **Awareness and Action: A Resource Book on Anti-Semitism** published by the New Jewish Agenda; **Networking for Women** published by the Israel Women's Network; **Bridges, "A Journal for Jewish Feminists and our Friends";** and **Lilith: The Jewish Women's Magazine.**

Through the months of writing we have discovered and strengthened our personal and collective voices. We have come to own the fullness of our lives, the pain, the joy, the sorrow, the laughter. We give this book to you now as our gift. "Use it in good health."

Janet Carnay
Laura Wine Paster
Marcia Cohn Spiegel

February 28, 1992
Palos Verdes, California

# INTRODUCTION

*The Jewish Women's Awareness Guide* is a starting place for Jewish women of all ages to get together in groups—to look at our past as a way of understanding our present and planning for the future. We need only bring ourselves, our personal experiences, our histories, our personal feelings and intuitions and our personal truths. This *Guide* is meant to give women a way to talk to each other on a new level, openly, honestly and without judgment.

It is important that we understand the opportunities and limits of these groups. *These are not therapy groups;* they are not support groups, although there will be an element of support in them; they are not classes although we will certainly learn from each other; they are not gripe sessions; they are not problem-solving groups.*

They *are* groups in which we will look at the forces that have shaped us as Jewish women. We will try to understand how the many different messages we receive influence our perceptions of ourselves. We will discover how much we have in common as well as how unique we are. We will recognize that we are not alone.

---

*It is a good idea for the group to be aware of community resources to turn to or use as a back-up for emotional support. e.g. Jewish Family Service Agencies, women's or campus counseling center, Twelve-Step programs such as Alanon (for families of alcoholics), ACOA (for adult children of alcoholics) and CODA (Co-dependents Anonymous), etc. Note: If you are now in therapy or counseling, we strongly advise you to show this material to your therapist or counselor before making a commitment to the group.

## Why a Group

By answering the questions in the *Guide* on your own, you will learn a lot about yourself, but by listening to other women in a group responding to the same questions, you will learn about their lives, and more about your own life as well. Equally important is what you will learn about the condition of being a woman and being a Jew. Sharing thoughts about your life in a group which you trust helps you to find your voice and the courage to speak your truth. Whether or not you are a member of a group, you may want to use the questions as the basis for a personal journal. You may want to discuss the questions with your family or partner as a way to talk about the past and your different memories and experiences. However you choose to use this *Guide,* we hope that it will be helpful in your journey of self-discovery.

### A. Starting an Awareness Group

There are several ways to begin. An *Awareness Group* may be an activity of Hillel, a synagogue sisterhood or other existing organization. Or a group of women friends and acquaintances may come together to talk about their lives. Or one woman may put notices in the local newspaper, bulletin boards and Jewish publications to seek out other women to start a new group. We have found that it is important for women to understand the distinctive and different nature of these groups. A description like this one which we have used may be helpful to you to attract potential members.

**By responding to questions in group discussion, women will look at the forces that have shaped their lives and the many different messages that have influenced their perceptions of themselves. In particular, the series will focus on women's relationships and the impact of our culture of Jewish women's self-image.**

It is not necessary or even desirable for all the women in the group to be friends. Some of the most successful groups are made up of women who did not know each other before the group began. Groups do not have to be made up of women all the same age, all married or all single, all straight or all lesbian, all in school or all working, etc. Being Jewish women is what we have in common, and the purpose of the group is to discover what that means.

## B. The Demonstration Meeting

If you are the person who is initiating the *Awareness Group,* you will need to become familiar with the *Guide* in order to conduct the demonstration exercise and describe the material to the other women.

At this first get-together, after everybody has introduced themselves, you, as the facilitator, will talk about the content of the *Guide* and the opportunity to look at our lives in a new way. Following the "Demonstration Exercise,"* women should take time to look through the *Guide* to see if they would be interested in continuing an ongoing awareness group.

In our experience women may not be ready to make such a commitment at this stage. Because the question in the *Guide* will touch areas of sensitivity for all women, we suggest that those who are interested meet two more times to discuss the questions of the first two chapters, *In the Beginning* and *Family and Friends* and examine the questions in the other chapters. At this time there should be a sense of what the material is like; whether there is a wish to continue and which chapters are of particular interest.

## C. Planning the Group

How large will the group be? Seven to ten women is a good number for a beginning. This allows for a diversity of life experiences and opinions and small enough to allow each woman ample time to respond to questions. If your group is larger, we recommend that you divide into smaller groups.

How often will the group meet? Weekly, bi-weekly, etc.
When will the group meet?
Where will the group meet? Homes, classroom, synagogue, library, etc.

How long should each meeting last? In our experience, 2½ hours seems to be a minimum.

How many meetings will there be? We would suggest a series of four to six, at which time the group can decide if all wish to continue.

Which topics will the group do? As already suggested, the first two chapters are a good place to begin. Although the Guide was written in a particular order, your group may choose any chapters you wish, in any order.

Who will facilitate the meetings? The group works best when each person takes a turn as the facilitator. (See The Facilitator)

Who can attend meetings? In order to build trust and to assure confidentiality, it is a good idea to limit attendance to members of the group and to discourage visitors and drop-ins.

### D. How the Group Decides

How will the group make its decisions? e.g. how many meetings, which topics, etc. We have found the best way to insure that everyone feels that she has an equal say in the group decision is to use a short, simple process called "The Delphi System". Using this method no one is forced to make only one choice; each woman can vote for all the options that she likes.

1. At the meeting the facilitator writes down the choices to be voted on. e.g. which chapters to discuss for future sessions.

2. She reads aloud all of the choices and then gives the group a moment to consider which they prefer.

3. All vote on each item. Each one votes by holding up fingers—5 fingers for those items you are the *most* interested in, 4 for those you strongly like, 3 for those of moderate interest, 2, 1 or none for those you like less or have no interest in. You can vote 5 on as many items as you like, or 4 or 3, etc. reflecting your choice about each item.

4. The facilitator reads an item and all vote on it (as described in #3 above). The

13

facilitator "counts fingers", arrives at a total and announces it to the group. She does the same for each item on the list.

5. The group looks at the totals and eliminates those chapters that have the least number of votes. If the remaining number of chapters is more than the group wants, repeat the voting process with these remaining chapters.

When this process is completed, the results will truly reflect the thinking of each member of the group. No one will feel left out. For those who have never tried it, "The Delphi System" may sound complicated, but it really is not. It is simple and it includes everyone's opinion. You will also find this system useful in certain chapters in this book, particularly *Control of our Bodies* and *Into Action.*

E. Ground Rules for Groups

1. It is important to establish trust and strict confidentiality. This means that nothing that others say in the group should be discussed anywhere else, at any time—at home, with family or friends, even your closest confidant. This is the basic requirement to build trust in the group. Of course, you may share your own feelings and discoveries with someone close to you.

2. We show our support for the group by always arriving on time, staying for the entire meeting, and finishing on time.

3. We show our respect and caring by giving each other undivided attention and listening to each other without judgment. We talk only about our own experiences and only when it is our turn to talk. It is important not to interrupt others, even to comment "I know just how you feel". Making suggestions, solving problems or trying to fix things for someone else doesn't work in a group like this. Sentences that begin "If only you had . . ." or "You should have . . ." cause pain to the listener and sound judgmental.

4. Because we want to give our undivided attention, only one person speaks at a time. There are no side conversations, note-taking, doodling, knitting, needlepoint, etc.

14

5. To allow everyone her chance to be heard, we each speak only when it is our turn. No one is ever required to reply to a question, and may choose to pass or refrain from speaking by saying "I pass," "I'd rather not answer," or a similar phrase. However, if you do "pass," you may choose to speak after every one else has had her turn.

6. Your responsibility as a group member is to be aware that time is limited and there are many things to say. Each of our stories is important and we each need to have a turn to speak. If the facilitator reminds you that your time is up, it is never personal, but insures that each woman has her chance to speak and be heard.

7. In talking about our lives, our own experiences are valid in and of themselves. We don't need to bring in opinions from books or outside authorities, such as our teachers, parents, partners or rabbis, etc.* It is helpful to tell our stories in the first person, "I saw", "I thought", "I felt".

8. Being an active member of the group means taking your turn as the facilitator.

9. Expect the unexpected.

## F. The Facilitator

1. The role of the facilitator is to help the group participate fully in the discussion. She insures that each person has an opportunity to speak; she keeps the discussion on track in terms of time and content, and by her example, shows the group how to listen attentively and without judgment.

The facilitator is not a therapist, a director, or authority figure. She does not control the group, solve problems, or fix things. Some of this material will cause emotional responses; it is okay for people

*Recommended Readings at the back of the *Guide* are for individual later follow-up, if so desired.

to cry. She trusts her intuition in dealing with this situation. She doesn't minimize a problem or pretend it is not serious; she accepts the intense feelings that the person is experiencing and encourages her to share her feelings until she is able to become calm. When the facilitator feels that it is time to return to the discussion, she asks the person involved if she is ready to continue.

2. She prepares herself for the session she is leading by careful reading of the chapter and thinking about how she will reply, in order to anticipate the responses from the group and be sensitive to the emotional content of the question. The facilitator also responds to the questions as an equal member of the group. If she starts by calling on someone two or three seats away from her to begin, her own answer will come early in the discussion, giving her an opportunity to set the tone. She watches the time to insure that each member has enough time to speak, guides the group back to the topic if the discussion wanders, and also reminds the group of their agreement of confidentiality and of being non-judgmental.

3. She is gentle but firm in handling the excessive talker, the advice giver, the interrupter, the argumentative person and the one who judges others. She may do this by repeating the question, reminding the group of the *Ground Rules for the Group* or restating the time limit, all in a friendly tone.

4. There may not always be time to cover every question. At the halfway point the facilitator looks to see how much of the material has been covered. If it appears that there will not be enough time to do everything, she can ask the group if they would like to stay longer; if they want to add a special session to complete the questions; or if she should select some of the remaining questions for discussion. **In any event, each meeting should end with the *Closing Exercise.***

5. It is the facilitator's role to:

See that the room is set up so that people are sitting in a circle, able to make eye contact with each other.

Begin each meeting with introductions and reminder of the *Ground Rules* (E).

Be alert to group responses, and individual needs.
(Bring a box of Kleenex.)

Summarize after a question when a common thread is obvious.

Fifteen minutes before the end of the meeting she briefly summarizes her impression of the themes and "common threads" that have emerged from the discussion, and then asks others for their perceptions of the "common thread".

## G. The Order of Business

*Seating should be in a circle. Begin and end on time.*

This is a suggested format for each get-together of a group:

a. During the first few minutes of the meeting, the members of the group go around and share any feelings or thoughts they have about the previous get-together. Sometimes you may want to have a second go-round to encourage each woman to share something she did since the last meeting that made her feel good about herself.

b. Begin the topic by having someone read aloud the Introduction to the chapter.

c. The facilitator reads *The Opening Exercise* and each woman, incuding the facilitator, responds in turn. At any time a woman may choose not to answer. She can indicate that by saying "I pass," or "I'd rather not answer," or some other similar phrase. After everyone has had a chance to respond, the facilitator may want to return to the woman who "passed" to see if she would like to speak. The facilitator then proceeds to the other questions of the topic in the same way.

d. Fifteen minutes before the end of the meeting the facilitator and the group will summarize the impressions: finding the common threads that have emerged from the discussion. Following this summary, the group will do *The Closing Exercise.* Even if there is

17

not enough time to discuss every question, it is essential to do the closing exercise.

e. Finally before the group leaves, make announcements of any events which may be of interest to the members, and remind everybody about the time, place, facilitator and subject matter of the next meeting.

Hints for success:

The group works best if you address your answers to everyone, not only to the facilitator. Listen carefully to the question that is being asked and focus on your answer. Avoid lengthy stories; time is limited; there is much to be discussed.

Unexpected things will always happen in a group. We come with a wide range of emotions and life experiences which will cause us to respond quite differently to the same material. Part of our learning will be to accept the differences in our responses.

If someone gets upset or cries while answering a question, it is okay to reach out and offer her comfort. Don't try to talk her out of her feelings. Give her a chance to calm down before the group continues.

Some "extras" to consider:

Bringing old photos, letters, year books or other mementoes that relate to the theme of the chapter.

Reading books or articles that tie in to the theme. A list of recommended readings can be found at the back of the Guide.

Reading poems that tie in to the theme.

Playing or singing music that relates to the theme.

Doing an art or writing project that relates to the theme.

Seeing a movie, play, video or other performance.

Attending a synagogue service.

Attending a political event, rally or lecture.

(The group can decide when to incude any of these activities as part of a regular meeting or a special occasion devoted to creative expression.)

## H. Evaluating the Group

It is a good idea to stop periodically to evaluate your group's experience. (After the first two sessions, at the end of the initial series, if or when there are problems in the group, or when something unexpected happens, etc.) Here are some questions to think about in order to clarify your group experience. You might want to write down your thoughts for this discussion.

Has this been a satisfying experience for you? What has been most satisfying to you? How could it be better?

Do you feel connected to the group?

If you had a chance to be a facilitator, how did that feel? What did you like? What was difficult?

Has there been enough time to respond to the questions and get through the material? Do you feel that it would be helpful to have more than one meeting on a subject?

Are there other issues that you think should be discussed?

## I. Demonstration Exercise

This exercise is meant to experience a taste of what happens in a Jewish Women's Awareness group.

At this first meeting you may have more people than would normally attend. If there are more than 15 women present, we suggest you remain in one large group. The facilitator will then go part of the way around the group with the first question, and then change to the next question. In this way, everyone will have a chance to respond. Each woman in the circle should have a chance to take part in the opening and closing exercises. At later times when this large group is divided into several smaller ones, each woman will be able to respond to every question.

*Opening exercise: Can you remember a special time when you were glad that you were a woman? Can you describe it? Has there been a time when you regretted being a woman? Can you describe that time?*

1. Can you remember a time in your family when you felt that it was a problem being a girl? What made you feel this way? Can you remember a time in your family when you felt it was good to be a girl? What made you feel that way?

2. Can you remember a special time when you were glad that you were Jewish? Can you describe that time? Has there been a time when you were uncomfortable because you were Jewish? Can you describe that time?

3. Have you ever had an experience at school, at work, or in a volunteer organization when you felt it was a problem being Jewish and\or being a woman? What was it? How did this make you feel? What did you do?

*Closing exercise: What brought you to this group? What do you hope to get from this group?*

# USING THE GUIDE WITH YOUNG JEWISH WOMEN

We young women are in transition. From childhood to adulthood, choices and decisions challenge us, especially at this exciting and scary moment in our lives. While past decades have given new understanding of ourselves, there are many questions which we young Jewish women are only beginning to ask.

The primary function of this Guide is to empower us as Jewish women by exploring some basic questions. When we think of the special needs of young women, there is necessarily some generalizing, but whether young Jewish women are in college dorms, at work, or starting a family, there are many common concerns facing them.

## FORMING A GROUP

First, there is the need to associate with a group, "just like me," to find a place where one feels able to "be yourself." This Guide can become the instrument for forming a community where one feels at home as a Jewish woman, having common questions, fears and joys. On a college campus, women may want to build such a group. (Often a Jewish women's organization in your area might be willing to co-sponsor such an effort, or you may want to create a more intimate group by bringing together two or three of your friends to discuss thoughts and experiences using the Guide.)

A section could be adapted for a workshop at a conference relating to Jewish women studies, utilized to stimulate discussion in a classroom, or serve as a "one-shot" discussion or "rap session." Or, for example, a group of students interested in supporting Israel could use the topic, "Israel and Zionism" with its probing questions (Sec. III, No. 3) as the basis for an event. The topics in the Guide might be stimulating and helpful when read by an individual Jewish woman, not in a group, on her road to self-discovery.

With college campus groups, we have found the experience is more smooth if two things are kept in mind: A strong commitment to confidentiality; (group members are likely to have common friends and acquaintances) and second, a successful group is not necessarily comprised of "best friends". We have found it is not that one must like someone in order to support her. With all committed to a strong group, this can happen despite individual differences.

## CHOOSING TOPICS

While much thought has been given to the order in which the topics are considered, it is crucial that users be selective in choosing discussion topics. While all sections apply to most women to some degree, women at different stages and ages will be attracted to different topics.*

The first section, "The Personal Connection" is a good place to begin; but for young women, there may be more interest to start with the latter topics in that section and work backward. "Dreams, Hopes and Expectations, (No, 10) for example, deals with the future which is more a part of our immediate lives than are memories of childhood and early family relationships. One's past might be a more difficult topic to speak about with a group that does not yet feel comfortable together, even though it is essential at some time that women examine their own past.

A second topic would be Jewish Women and College (The Public Connection, II, No. 3.) Whether or not a woman is in college, it presents an opportunity to discuss what is most current in their lives, and would bring the group together if it is an on-campus group. If it is a mixed group of those who have and have not attended college, the idea of receiving a higher education has touched most Jewish young women's lives.

The next relevant topic might be one to introduce what it is to be a Jewish woman: how the world perceives us and how we see ourselves. This topic is well covered in Sec. II, No. 8, "The Media Mirror: How Jewish women are portrayed in movies and television." Before we can shift our awareness of what it means to be a Jewish woman, it is crucial to look at what images are made of the "typical Jewish woman"; how such images were formed and how they affect our self-judgment. For young women, it is especially important to explore our feelings about the term, "Jewish American Princess" as it may relate to our lives, as well as our experiences with, and our fears, of becoming stereotypical "Jewish mothers."

Possibly the single most important issue for all women, and especially for young women, is our feeling about our bodies and our sexuality. Because of the complexity of the topic, it is a good idea to discuss these three topics, either separately or in one long session: "The Woman in the Mirror: our body as image" (Sec. III No. 1), "Sex and the Jewish Woman: Ourselves as sexual beings", and "Control of our Bodies." (Sec. I, Nos. 7 & 8), The body image issue is one that is dealt with extensively on college campuses these days, and for good reason! To feel good about ourselves as women, it is essential we develop a satisfied attitude about our bodies. More than simply worrying about the size and shape of our torsos, as young Jewish women we often find ourselves dealing with issues of sexuality: having sex, sexual orientation, etc. This is an area which may be embarrassing to talk about but ought to be explored and shared with others. It is also important that sexuality is discussed in a "political" perspective. As young women, we should be able to discuss sexual assault and abortion rights as related to our own sexuality, so that we can stay strong and in control of our lives and our bodies.

Attitudes to money, class, authority and jobs, are probably as confusing to us as feelings about sexuality. Young people, Jews and women, each have separate "bags" of mixed emotions around each of those topics, so there may be much to define. We should consider "Money, and Power, Values and Class: how early attitudes influence our thinking and behavior" (Sec. I, No. 5), paying special attention to questions 7 through 10 about your present financial situation. Then take up "Authority and Control: how we feel about power and the people who wield it." (Sec. II, No. 7). In addition to the questions listed there, think about how you are treated as a young person and also as a young woman by people in authority and how you would like to see this change.

Developing a viewpoint toward money and authority, you may be ready to take up the topic of a job or a career. "What am I going to do for the rest of my life" and the issue of "how do I like where I am working now?" are considered in the section on "A Job or a Career: women at home and women at work," and "The Places We Work: Responding to our work environment." (Sec. II, Nos. 5 and 6)

The topics thus far mentioned are those we think absolutely necessary to young Jewish women. Beyond this, we leave choices to each individual or group. We suggest many may decide to discuss the general idea of women's community as formulated by "From Friendship Circles to the Women's Movement." (Sec. II, No. 1) This is especially relevant to women on campus who are looking to create a community-within-a-community and are struggling with their affiliations—how they mesh and intersect. Eventually, we should look at our past and see what has made us who we are today, with "Our Family and Friends" (Sec. I, no. 2) and discuss the relationships we had as we grew up. Another topic worth covering for all women is the chapter "From Chance to Choice" at the very end. This allows for a good wrap-up and for goal-setting for the future.

## ENJOYING THE GROUP

No matter which topics are covered, an important element to work for is FUN! In our experience, women in college and recent graduates tend to be trapped in an intellectual mindset from which they have difficulty escaping. It then becomes essential for thinking to be balanced with creative, spiritual and emotional outlets, lest the project grow boring and stale. Developing your own related projects and games; art, coloring, collage, weaving, masks, mural painting, sewing, are wonderful ways to express the proud Jewish woman you are. You may want also to share meals, take trips, watch movies and listen to speakers together, knitting the women in the group together.

Remember, *all* of the questions in each topic need not be asked or answered. "Go with the flow" as it takes you deeper into your understanding of yourself and of being a Jewish woman. Within our new-found communities, we must join together to reclaim our identity and release our power.

ABIGAIL WEINBERG
RUTH MAGDER

New York, NY 1992


We recommend women examine the entire Guide's contents first, especially the first 25 pages, also the Ground Rules and Facilitator material.

## I. The Personal Connection

"If I am not for myself, who will be for me?"

**1**

# In the Beginning

### Exploring our early experiences

As women we come together to share and explore the journeys of our lives. We begin with childhood memories that influenced how we grew up. We will recapture a sense of the Jewish girls we were in another time and another place.

*OPENING EXERCISE: Can you picture yourself as you were in grade school? Can you describe the trip you made to school each day? How old were you? Who did you go with and how did you get there? e.g. bus, car, walking.*

1. Can you describe your school in terms of where it was located and what the classrooms were like. Was it public or private, coeducational or single sex, religious or secular?

2. Who were your teachers? Were they men or women? Was the principal a man or a woman? Tell about a teacher you remember most vividly from school.

3. Do you remember what was it like to be a girl in your school? Did boys and girls play together at recess? Did they sit together in class? At lunch? Were there any activities that were only for boys or only for girls? Were you aware of any differences between the way boys and girls were treated? What were they?

4. What was it like to be Jewish in your grade school? What was the proportion of Jews? Were they a majority? A minority? Did you attend school on Jewish holidays? How did you feel about that? How were Christmas and Easter celebrated in your school? How did you feel about that?

5. Who were your friends in your neighborhood? Were they Jewish? Were they non-Jews? Were they boys or girls? What activities did boys and girls do together? What did you do only with girls? What did you want to do but could not because you were a girl? What did you want to do but could not because you were Jewish?

6. What was happening in the world at this time? e.g. Depression, war, civil rights movement, the 60's. How do you remember it?

7. Where did you go to high school? Describe the school in terms of the size and ethnic makeup of the student body, the ratio of girls to boys, Jews to non-Jews. Were your teachers men or women? Was the principal a man or a woman?

8. Do you remember what was it like to be a girl in your high school? Which activities were only for boys? Only for girls? What differences were you aware of between the way boys and girls were treated?

9. What groups were you in? e.g. social, study, organizations, and clubs. What were your feelings of belonging or not belonging? What was it like to be Jewish in your high school? Were there any activities or sports that were considered "not Jewish"? Did Jewish kids participate in student government, cheerleading, pep squads, etc.?

10. What were your activities outside of school at this time? e.g. work, social, cultural, religious. Which of these activities (including school) gave you the most satisfaction or pleasure?

*Closing exercise: If you could go back to that time and that place, who would you want to visit? What would you want to tell them? What would you want to ask them?*

# 2

# Family and Friends

## Relationships with important relatives and friends

In looking at ourselves today we are aware of the many facets of our lives. We have known times of joy and times of sorrow, times of love and times of loneliness. Each of our stories is unique; each of us has been shaped by a family history which we are about to explore.

As we begin to share we should remember our differences. Among us there may be women who were adopted, women who were raised in foster homes, women whose families were shattered by the Holocaust or other upheavals. As always it is up to each of us to decide whether or not to respond to a question.

*Opening exercise: Describe an early memory of a happy moment or incident in your family. Where were you? How old were you? Who was there?*

1. Where and when were you born? Who were you named for? Did you have sisters or brothers? What was the order of your birth?

2. What about your parents? Where and when were they born? How old were they when you were born? Was either married before? Widowed? Divorced? Did they have children from other marriages? Did you live with both your

parents while you were growing up? If not, what were the circumstances? e.g. separation, divorce, death. With which parent did you live

3. Where were your grandparents born? How did your family come to America? Where did they come from and where did they settle?

4. When you were a child where did your grandparents live? What language(s) did they speak at home? In public? How often did you see them? Describe a vivid memory you have of your grandparent(s) from that time.

5. Who were the relatives you and your parents spent the most time with during your childhood and what were the occasions? Who were the relatives you and your parents saw the least and what was your understanding of the reason for this?

6. What was an important family custom or ritual? e.g. birthdays, special songs or games, holiday celebrations, eating out, etc.

7. Who was the relative that you felt closest to during your childhood? What was the quality of that person that drew you to her/him?

8. What were your parents' feelings about, and observance, of Judaism as you were growing up? How was this different or similar to their parents? What tensions do you remember in your family around these issues?

9. Can you describe your family's attitude about non-Jews? About Blacks? About other people of color? Did they have non-Jewish friends? Who were your non-Jewish friends? Were you included in their holiday celebrations? How? How were they included in your holiday celebrations? Were there tensions in your family around relationships with non-Jews?

10. Were there any intermarriages in your family? Do you remember what your family said and did about these marriages?

11. Who are the family friends and relatives with whom you are still connected? What are the occasions when you get together?

*Closing exercise: Think back to a moment in your childhood when everything felt okay. What were you doing? Where were you? Who were you with?*

**3**

# Mothers and Daughters

Connecting our past with our present

As women, we are often aware of the impact of our mothers on our lives, without giving thought to the facts that shaped *their* personal histories. Today we will look at connections: grandmothers, mothers and daughters. Some of this material may be sensitive or long forgotten, particularly for those who have no memory of their mother or grandmother, or were raised by a stepmother or foster mother. As always it is up to each woman to decide whether or not to discuss a question.

*Opening exercise: You are visiting your mother when she was 16 years old. She is telling you about her hopes and dreams for the future. What does she want to be and what would she like to do?*

1. While she was growing up with whom did your mother live? Where? Was she the oldest? middle? youngest? What were the ages and sexes of other family members?

2. How far did your mother go in school? What was her first full time job and how old was she when she began to work?

3. How did your parents meet? What was your mother's life like at this time? How did her meeting your father change her life?

4. Looking back at your family life, can you remember what was expected of your mother with regard to the following:
- —taking care of the household, e.g. chores, shopping, repairs
- —working outside the home
  involvement in children's school and after-school activities
- —caring for family health
- —nurturing, e.g. affection, comfort and consolation, support and protection, etc.
- —expressing Jewish values and traditions

Where did these expectations come from? herself? parents? spouse\partner? children? Jewish community?

5. Which of these activities do you think gave your mother the greatest pleasure? What did she complain about?

6. What did your mother do that you think she was most proud of? What do *you* think was her biggest regret?

7. Do you know what your mother did that *her* mother was most proud of? Do you know what your mother did that was most disappointing to *her* mother? What problems do you think your mother had with her mother?

8. Do you know how your mother got along with her mother-in-law? Were there problems between them?

9. How did you get along with your mother's mother? What was your relationship like? Was it the same or different with your father's mother?

10. What do you think your mother expected of you? e.g. your goals, your responsibility to the family, education, marriage, etc. What were her expectations of you as a Jewish woman? What have you done that your mother is\was most proud of? What have you done that was most disappointing to her?

11. Can you remember a moment when you caught yourself acting just like your mother? What were you doing?

12. For those women who have daughters, describe a moment when you saw yourself in your daughter(s).

13. What do you and your daughter(s) do together that gives you the greatest pleasure?

14. Do you think being Jewish has influenced the relationship between you and your mother? Between you and your daughter(s)? How? e.g. expectations, respect, closeness, nurturing, etc.

15. What part of your mother's personality or character do you admire or respect the most? What part of your relationship with your mother has been the most disappointing to you?

16. With respect to your mother's past history and actions, how was she able to make choices and\or how was she limited by circumstances over which she had no control?

*Closing exercise: If you could give a gift to your mother what would it be?*
*If your mother could give a gift to you what would you want it to be?*
*If you could give a gift to your daughter what would it be?*

**4**

# Finding our Fathers

Searching for connection with the first man in
our lives.

As we become aware of the pieces of our past which have
made us who we are, it becomes obvious that our fathers,
whether present or absent, have played a prominent role. In
looking at the past we shall try to understand the forces
that shaped our fathers' lives and how our lives, in turn,
have been influenced by our fathers.

*Opening exercise: You are visiting your father when he was
16 years old. He is telling you about his hopes and dreams
for the future. What does he want to be and what would he
like to do?*

1. While he was growing up with whom did your father
live? where? Was he the oldest? middle? youngest? What
were the ages and sexes of other family members?

2. How far did your father go in school? What was his first
full-time job and how old was he when he began to work?
Was he in the armed services? Where and when did he
serve? How did this affect his life?

3. What do you know about your father's life when he met
your mother? How did his life change as a result of their
meeting?

4. Looking back at your family life, can you remember what was expected of your father with regard to the following:

  —taking care of the household, e.g. chores, shopping, repairs
  —working outside the home
  —involvement in children's school and after school activities
  —caring for family health
  —nurturing, e.g. affection, comfort and consolation, support and protection, etc.
  —expressing Jewish values and traditions

Where did these expectations come from? himself? parents? spouse/partner? children? Jewish community?

5. Which of these activities do you think gave your father the greatest pleasure? What did he complain about?

6. What did your father do that you think he was most proud of? What do you think was his biggest regret?

7. Do you know what your father did that *his* mother was most proud of? Do you know what your father did that was most disappointing to *his* mother? What problems do you think your father had with his mother?

8. Do you know how your father got along with his mother-in-law? Were there problems between them?

9. What do you think your father expected of you? e.g. your goals, your responsibility to the family, education, marriage, etc. What were his expectations of you as a Jewish woman? What have you done that your father is/was most proud of? What have you done that was most disappointing to him?

10. Can you remember a moment when you caught yourself acting just like your father? What were you doing?

11. For those women who have sons, describe a moment when you saw yourself in your son(s).

12. What do you and your son(s) do together that gives you the greatest pleasure?

13. Do you think being Jewish has influenced the relationship between you and your father? Between you and your son(s)? How? e.g. expectations, respect, closeness, nurturing, etc.

14. What part of your father's personality or character do you admire or respect the most? What part of your relationship with your father has been the most disappointing to you?

15. With respect to your father's past history and actions, how was he able to make choices and/or how was he limited by circumstances over which he had no control?

*Closing exercise: If you could give a gift to your father what would it be?*
*If your father could give a gift to you what would you want it to be?*
*If you could give a gift to your son what would it be?*

# 5

# Money and Power, Values and Class

## Attitudes that influence our thinking and actions

The vision of entering a classless society drew generations of Jewish immigrants to the New World. They believed that any individual could aspire to a life of material comfort in *Die Goldene Medina* (The Golden Land). Although some of us succeeded far beyond our dreams, others of us have not yet made those dreams a reality. And yet we still tend to see ourselves as members of a vast middle class in a system of equality. It is painful for us to feel that we have more than others, and it may be even more painful for us to feel that we have less. Because of this we are uncomfortable acknowledging class differences. For many of us there is more shame in talking about class and money than there is in talking about sex. When we do talk about "class" we mean more than money; we usually include ideas about where we live, what we wear, our jobs or careers, our leisure time, the schools we attend, etc. Each of us started at a different place; each of us has taken a different path to reach this moment; each of us will answer these questions differently. There are no good answers or bad answers, just the truths of our lives.

*Opening exercise: Reflecting back to fifth grade, how*

*would you describe your neighborhood in terms of family income? e.g. working class, middle class, upper class. How did your family fit in?*

1. Describe your neighborhood in terms of the following: apartments\private homes, own\rent, ethnic and religious mix, occupations, cars, kinds of stores, etc.

2. Describe your family at that time. What kind of work did your parents or other immediate family members do? What was the attitude about mothers going to work? Staying home? Did you have household help? A car? Where did you go on vacations? Summer camp? Did you have private lessons of any kind? Did you wear hand-me-down clothes?

3. At that time in your life and during your teen years, how did you feel compared to your friends? What differences were there between you? e.g. room of your own\shared room, clothes, spending money, after-school activities, etc.

4. What was your parents' attitude toward money? e.g. earning it, spending it, donating it, investing it, displaying it? In what situations did you think they were inconsistent? How did this make you feel?

5. Who was in charge of money in your family? Who paid the bills? Who signed the checks? Who decided how money would be spent? Were there conversations and\or arguments over money? What were they? Did your parents talk to you about their finances? How did you feel about this? How did *you* get money? Was this the same for both boys and girls in your family?

6. What was the connection in your family between money and being Jewish? e.g. belonging to a synagogue, Jewish center or country club, fund raising for Jewish organizations, giving charity (tzedakah)?

7. In your life now how do *you* get money? e.g. from parents, from spouse, from your earnings.

8. To what degree are you now in control of your income and expenses? How does this make you feel? Do you think

being a woman causes difficulties in controlling your money? How? e.g. earning money, getting credit, men\ women issues, family budgets, etc.

9. How do you feel about asking someone in your family for money? e.g. parents, spouse\partner, children. Are there current tensions around the subject of money in your family? What are they? Do you feel someone in your family is judging how you spend your money? Who is it and what is the message?

10. How would you describe your current attitude toward money? e.g. earning it, spending it, donating it, investing it, displaying it? How is this the same or different from your parents?

11. On what kind of things do you find it easy to spend money? On what kind of things is it difficult? How does this affect your life?

12. Which of these or similar situations have you had to deal with?

—Being rejected or rejecting someone because of a lack of money or difference in economic level, income or class?
—Pursuing someone or being pursued because of money or class?
—Breaking off a relationship or marriage because one partner earns more than the other, or not enough?
—Having significant problems or ending a relationship because of different values on how to spend money?

13. When you meet other women, what are you aware of about them? e.g. profession, clothes, home, cars, household help, nannies, hairdo and make-up, mannerisms, etc? What do you assume about them?

14. When you meet other Jews, are you aware of the same things. Different things? What are your assumptions and conclusions about them?

15. What is the common stereotype of Jews and money? Where have you encountered this attitude? In your own experience how true is this stereotype?

*Closing exercise: How do you see your economic status now? How has it changed since your childhood? How do you expect it to change in the future?*

# 6

# Having Fun

Vacation, recreation and leisure time

Earlier generations of Jews, struggling to survive in a hostile environment, did not have the luxury of leisure and recreation. Their lives were focused on earning a living, putting food on the table and raising a family. The cycle of Jewish life gave them a break from their daily activities: the observance of Sabbath, the celebration of holidays and the rare chance to dance joyously at a wedding. Because our grandmothers and their mothers had little time for relaxation, we have virtually no history of how Jewish women had fun. As we have become more affluent we have more time for leisure, and assimilation has provided us with new models.

*Opening exercise: When you were a little girl what did you do with your family to have fun?*

1. When you were in elementary school what did you like to do in your free time?:

   —Hobbies (collecting, creating art, experimenting with science, etc)
   —Sports
   —Clubs and\or scouting
   —Jewish center and\or synagogue activities

41

—Street games (ball, tag, etc.)
—Outdoor play (bikes, skating, jump rope, etc.)
—Indoor play (board games, puzzles, cards, dolls, etc.)
—Reading
—Watching TV

What did you do alone? What did you do with friends? What did you do with family?

2. What "special" activities did you do with your friends? e.g. sleepovers, slumber parties, trips, birthday parties, etc.

3. What activities did you want to be part of but could not? Why? e.g. parent(s) did not approve, not for girls, not Jewish, too expensive, you weren't chosen, you weren't physically able, etc.

4. What activities did your parent(s) make you do that you didn't want to do? Why? How did that make you feel then? How do you feel about it now?

5. What activities did you do where you felt pressure to perform? From whom? e.g. parent(s), team mates, friends, teachers, coach, etc. How did this affect your experience of those activities? How does this affect you now?

6. Do you remember what your parent(s) did to have fun? What was it? How did they have fun with their friends? Other family members?

7. Did your family go on vacations together? Where did they go? e.g. Jewish resort, camping, traveling, visiting relatives. Did you look forward to these vacations? What was disappointing?

8. Did you go away to camp? Was it a Jewish camp? Was it a girls' camp or for boys and girls? What did you like about camp? What didn't you like?

9. When you were a teenager, what did you like to do in your free time? What activities did you want to be part of but could not? Why?

10. Regarding leisure activities and sports, which do you

consider to be "Jewish"? Which do you consider to be non-Jewish? Which are okay for women? Which are not okay for women?

11. What do you like to do *now* in your free time? What do you like to do when you are alone? With others? What did you do *for yourself* that was fun this week? This month? This year?

12. What activities would you want to do but cannot? Why? What activities have you tried but stopped? What were they and why did you not continue?

*Closing exercise: If you could plan a very special vacation, with no restrictions of money, time or responsibility, where would you go? Who would you take with you? What would you do?*

# The Woman in the Mirror

## Our body as image

Once upon a time there was a princess with perfect features and a perfect body. She was so beautiful that she never felt sad or scared. She found true love and she lived happily ever after!

And then there are the rest of us, *real* women with *real* bodies who continually judge ourselves on the basis of images from the media, the fashion industry, and the men and women in our lives. No woman in our culture can avoid the feelings of inadequacy or imperfection that come from comparing ourselves to these images. We are all victims of the illusion that by looking and dressing a certain way, we can achieve true love and happiness. Those of us who don't fit the image pay the painful price daily of self-criticism and self-doubt. By exploring together our feelings about our bodies and where these feelings come from, we will help each other move toward a more positive self-image.

*Opening exercise: Pretend you are standing naked in front of a full-length mirror. Which parts of your body do you look at first? Which parts of your body do you avoid looking at?*

1. When you were a child, can you remember how modesty and nakedness were treated in your family? By your par-

ent(s)? By your sister(s)? By your brother(s)? Others in your home?

2. When you were a child, who did your family say you looked like? Which of your physical features were the subject of discussion? Teasing? Comparison? Judgment? How did that make you feel?

3. Can you remember how you felt about your body when you were 8 years old? What judgments did you make about your body? What did peers and other people say about your body?

4. When your body began to change how did you feel about it? What judgments did you make about your body? What did your family members say about your body? What comparisons did your girlfriends make regarding your body? What judgments did boys make about your body?

5. As a teenager what was your "ideal" of female beauty? e.g. hair, nose, bust, hips, legs, etc. How did you think you measured up to this standard of beauty? What did or would you have changed about yourself to fit your ideal?

6. As a teenager, what was your idea of "looking Jewish"? How did you think you did or did not fit the stereotype? In regard to this stereotype, what did you change or what would you have wanted to change about the way you looked?

7. In your life now what do you do for your body that makes you feel good? e.g. manicure, massage, exercise, hair care, etc. Describe a time when you felt really good about your body.

8. In your life now what do you do for your body as a response to the messages from others (media, family, partner, men, Jewish community, friends, work)? How do you feel about women's use of deodorants, shaving or waxing body hair, plucking or waxing facial hair, changing hair style or color, dieting etc.?

9. How do you decide what clothes and accessories to buy

and wear? What has influenced these choices? e.g. cost, friends, partner, men, family, Jewish community, fashion magazines, media, image you would like to project, etc.

10. Which of these or similar situations have you had to deal with:

—Being rejected or rejecting someone because of your looks or their looks?
—Pursuing someone or being pursued because of looks or image?
—Having a significant problem or breaking off a relationship or marriage because one partner doesn't meet the standards or expectations of the other with regard to looks?

11. In your life today which of the following are you comfortable with and which create discomfort?

—Shopping for a bathing suit
—Shopping for an outfit for a special occasion
—Eating dessert
—Gaining weight
—Losing weight
—Being photographed
—Accepting compliments about how you look
—Nursing in public or seeing someone nurse in public
—Tattooing
—Piercing—ears, nose, lips, etc.

How have these levels of comfort and discomfort been influenced by messages from your parents? Your friends? Men? The Jewish community?

12. As your body changes and ages what do you look forward to? What do you fear? e.g. wrinkles, grey hair, sagging breasts, bulging stomach, health problems, etc. How do\will you attempt to hide the signs of aging?

*Closing exercise: Finish this story—*
*Once upon a time there was a wonderful world where women controlled the media, the fashion industry and entertainment. You had the freedom to wear whatever you wanted, you could look whatever way you wanted, you could eat whatever you wanted. So you made the following choices—*

# 8

# Sex and the Jewish Woman

## Ourselves as sexual beings

We begin once more from the child's point of view to deal with a subject, which for most of us was forbidden, secret or never voiced. When we were young girls developing physically and sexually, our natural curiosity was often met with anxiety or shame. Even now, as grown women we may carry within us some of these old feelings of discomfort in talking about our sexuality. For women with disabilities and for lesbian and bisexual women, there may be additional areas of discomfort. The questions in this chapter are intended to explore the common threads in our lives as women. By sharing our experiences here we continue to create the bonds and connections among us.

*Opening exercise: When you were a little girl what words did you and your family use for vagina, penis, breasts, buttocks, intercourse, menstruation?*

1. Do you remember how old you were when you first had questions about sex? Who did you go to and what was the response?

2. Do you remember if your parent(s) ever started a conversation with you about sex? What was the occasion? Did any later conversations take place?

3. What did you learn about sex from what your parent(s)

said to you? From what they said to others? What did you learn about sexuality from observing your parent(s)? What did you learn about affection from observing your parent(s)?

4. Can you remember an experience from your childhood in which you became aware of sexuality? e.g. playing with friends, seeing something explicitly sexual, touching or being touched, etc. Can you remember a time when you were aware of feeling sexually different from your friends (other girls, boys)?

5. When did your body begin to change? i.e. breasts develop, growth of pubic and body hair. Was this earlier, later or at the same time as your friends? Do you remember how you felt about these changes? How did your family react?

6. At what age did you begin to menstruate? Was this earlier, later or at the same time as your friends? What did you know about menstruation before your first period? How did you find out? How did you feel about getting your period? How did your family react?

7. When you were a teenager did you know anything about the Jewish laws of family purity (menstruation, intercourse, ritual bath)? Did this information affect your attitude about your sexuality?

8. As a teenage girl what messages about sex did you receive from your parents with regard to:

—How you dressed (clothes, hair, makeup)
—Who you went out with
—What you could talk about
—What you read and watched (magazines, t.v., films)
—How you presented your body (posture, dancing, movements)
—What was allowable sexual behavior (virginity, birth control, making out, petting—in private? in public?)

What messages did you receive from your friends? From the Jewish community?

9. How were these attitudes (in question 8) different for your Jewish girl friends? Your non-Jewish girl friends? Your brother(s)? Jewish boys? Non-Jewish boys?

10. When you were a teenager, who was your ideal of sexual desirability? e.g. media star, teacher or relative, school celebrity. What woman? What man?

11. As an adult who is your ideal of sexual desirability? What woman? What man? What characteristics do you find sexually desirable? e.g. personality, body type, hair color, Jewish, non-Jewish, age.

12. Has your sense of yourself as a sexual person been influenced by these images? Has your choice of sexual partner(s) been influenced by them?

13. In your life today which of these are you comfortable with and which upset you or make you anxious?

—Dating
—Wearing clothes than enhance your sexuality
—Close physical contact (dancing, hugging, massage)
—Virginity
—Celibacy
—Talking about sex with other women? with men? with your children? with your parents?
—Expressing to your sexual partner what gives you pleasure? What you don't like? What you would like to change?
—Looking at or reading pornography alone? With your sexual partner? With a group?
—Erotic fantasies
—Masturbation
—Orgasm
—Oral sex
—Anal sex
—Use of sexual aids
—Varying sexual positions

14. To what degree do you think your comfort or discom-

fort reflects the attitudes of your parents? Your friends? Men? The Jewish community?

*Closing exercise: If the little girl you once were came to you now with her questions, fears and curiosity about sex, what would you tell her? How would you reassure her?*

# 9

# Shalom Bayit (Peace in the House): Fact or Fiction

## Our family emotions, past and present

The concept of *Shalom Bayit* (Peace in the House), is based on the idea that God is seeking peace in the heavens, between the nations on earth, and particularly between husband and wife. Ancient sources tell us that "the ultimate achievement of peace on earth depends upon its achievement in the smallest social unit—the family."*

This ancient ideal of reconciliation has permeated the lives of Jewish families for centuries. Although we may not know the phrase *"Shalom Bayit"*, our behavior reflects the expectation of this tradition. We feel the need to conceal from the world and, often, even from ourselves, the discord and disharmony that occurs within our homes. In some families the price of keeping peace at any cost can be repression of our true feelings and denial of real problems. In other families our inability to achieve *Shalom Bayit* creates feelings of shame and isolation. Some of these issues may have been kept behind closed doors; as we open these doors we let in light to see more clearly what was once in the dark.

*Opening exercise: Thinking back to your childhood, can*

---

*Encyclopedia Judaica, Jerusalem: Keter, 1971, Volume 14, Page 1356.

*you describe a "typical" family meal. Who was there? What do you remember that was pleasant? What do you remember that was unpleasant?*

1. Do you remember how you were expected to behave at family meals? Was this different for other girls in your family? Boys? Adults? What happened when you didn't behave as expected? How did you feel about this? How did you react?

2. Did you have a choice about what you ate? Were you ever forced to eat things you didn't like? Was food used as a reward and/or punishment? How did you feel about this and how did you react?

3. As a child what choices were you allowed to make with regard to:

  —What you wore
  —How you fixed your hair
  —How you spent your own money
  —How your room looked
  —Who your friends were—Jewish, non-Jewish
  —How you spent your free time
  —How much TV you watched
  —How much time you spent on the phone

How did you feel about these choices or limitations? How did you react? How were these different from your sister(s)? Brother(s)? Friends?

4. When you were a child what room did you sleep in? Who did you share a room with? What was your private space in this room? To what extent were you able to have privacy? e.g. closing doors, talking on the phone, friends visiting, diary, mail, etc. How did this make you feel? Were there rules for keeping your room clean? Were there consequences for not following the rules?

5. As a child what role(s) did you play in your family? e.g.

good girl, bad girl, little mother, the princess, funny girl, the brat, the brain, the scapegoat, the victim, the perfect child, responsible girl, etc. What role(s) did your sister(s) play? What role(s) did your brother(s) play? How did these roles change when you were a teenager? When you were an adult?

6. When you had conflicts with your sister(s) and brother(s) how were they settled? Did you and your sister(s) and brother(s) fight? What did you fight about? How did you fight? e.g. teasing, name-calling, yelling, hitting, etc. How did this make you feel? What did your parent(s) do when you fought?

7. When your parent(s) had a conflict how was it settled? Who did your parent(s) fight with? What did your parent(s) fight about? How did they fight? What did you do when your parent(s) fought? Do you remember how you felt about their fighting?

8. Do you remember if your father said things to you about your mother? What did he say? Do you remember if your mother said things to you about your father? What did she say? Did you feel that you were expected to choose sides in their disagreements? How did this make you feel? How did you react?

9. When you were a child how were the following expressed in your family?

| Happiness | Anger |
| Sadness | Fear |
| Rage | Joy |
| Love | Anxiety |
| Hatred | Jealousy |
| Approval | Disapproval |
| Shame | |

By your mother? By your father? By your sister(s)? By your brother(s)?

10. When you were a child how were you rewarded and\or praised? Who praised you? Do you remember a time that you deserved praise or reward and did not receive it? Who did you want it from? How did this change when you were a teenager?

11. When you were a child what were you punished for? How were you punished? Who punished you? How was this different for your sister(s)? Your brother(s)? How did this change when you were a teenager? As an adult looking back do you feel the punishments were fair?

12. In your family who did you turn to for nurturing? Support? Advice? Who do you turn to now?

13. When you were a teenager what was your image of Jewish family life with regard to the following?

—How family members treated each other
—How Jewish mothers behaved
—How Jewish fathers behaved
—Expectations of success
—Role in the Jewish community
—Abuse of drugs—prescription, non-prescription, street drugs
—Abuse of alcohol (becoming alcoholic)
—Incest
—Child abuse
—Battering spouses
—Uncontrollable rage
—Gambling
—Adultery
—Use of guns

Did you know any Jewish families who did not fit this

image? What was the image these families presented to the Jewish community?

14. How old were you when you felt you were an adult? At that time how did your family respond? In what ways are you now treated as an adult? In what ways are you still treated as a child? How does that make you feel? How did they act when you moved away from home? How did you feel when you moved away from home?

15. How do you think your experiences in your family affect your attitude toward relationships? e.g. dating, friendships, marriage\partnership, parenting, in-laws, etc.

16. What positive values and\or experiences did you gain in your family that you would like to pass on to others?

*Closing exercise: We close this session with a traditional Jewish blessing, a prayer for going on our way, T'filat Haderech\*\*. As we have journeyed together into our past, and now return to the present, we read aloud this blessing for peace.*

> *May we be blessed as we go on our way*
> *May we be guided in peace*
> *May we be blessed with health and joy*
> *May this be our blessing, Amen*
>
> *May we be sheltered by the wings of peace*
> *May we be kept in safety and in love*
> *May grace and compassion find their way to every*
>     *soul*
> *May this be our blessing, Amen*

---

\*\*Translation from the Hebrew by Debbie Friedman, copyright 1990, Sounds Write Production, Inc.

## 10

# Dreams, Hopes and Expectations

## Our lives today

There was a time when Jewish women knew what was expected of them: they would grow up, get married and have children; they would cook, keep a Jewish home, maintain traditions and take care of their husbands and families. This was the way things were supposed to be. This was the formula for happiness. But even then, for those who followed the formula exactly, there were no guarantees of happiness. Today women have moved beyond a single simple formula. They can now choose to live alone, to live with a woman or a man, to marry or not, to have a career or not, to have children or not. Some women have dared to take risks, to change their lifestyle, to juggle family, relationship, career, and more. And yet, there are still no guarantees of happiness. It is only when we define for ourselves our dreams and hopes that we can discard the old expectations. Then we can accept ourselves: our struggles, our strengths, our weaknesses.

*Opening exercise: In your life what have you ever done or accomplished that you thought you couldn't do?*

1. What did you learn about yourself from this experience? Who encouraged and/or supported you in this accomplish-

ment? How was your achievement acknowledged by you? By others?

2. In your life what have you ever wanted to do or accomplish that you didn't try to do? What stood in your way?

3. What have you done or accomplished that your family wanted you to do? What have you done or accomplished that your family did not want you to do? What have you wanted to do or accomplish that you didn't try to do because of your family?

4. What is expected of you in your family? e.g. dating/or marrying a "nice Jewish boy", excelling in your studies or career, having children, visiting your family often, etc.

5. How do you define "being single"? What do you think is pleasurable about being single? What do you think is difficult? How does being single affect the way you feel about yourself? How does being single affect the way your family responds to you? Does being a single woman interfere with doing things you want to do? How?

6. How do you define "being in a relationship"? What do you think feels good about being in a relationship? What do you think is difficult? How does being in a relationship affect the way you feel about yourself? How does being in a relationship affect the way your family responds to you? Does being a woman in a relationship interfere with doing things you want to do? How?

7. What do you enjoy doing just for yourself? e.g. taking time off, treating yourself to something wonderful, going to a favorite place, etc. How do you feel when you do something for yourself?

8. What do you enjoy doing for others (friends, partner, family) that's special? e.g. cooking a favorite dish, getting or making a special gift, celebrating birthdays or other events, etc.

9. In relationships with others (friends, partner, family) how comfortable do you feel doing the following:

—initiating contact (phone, visit, mail)
—inviting them to your home
—inviting them to an outside event (concert, movie, picnic, etc)
—calling to chat
—arranging special events (seders, birthday parties, showers, etc)
—helping them in times of crisis
—expressing hurt and anger to them
—sharing good news
—talking about intimate problems
—calling or visiting because it is your duty

10. In regard to the list above, what do you expect from your friends, partner and family? How do you let them know what you expect of them? How do you feel when they don't meet your expectations? What do you do? e.g. tell them, let it go, feel depressed, get angry, etc.

*Closing exercise: If your dreams could become reality, what would you want to accomplish? What would your relationships be like? How would you like to feel about yourself?*

## II. The Public Connection

"If I am only for myself, what am I?"

# 1

# From Friendship Circles to Feminism

## Women-to-women: home and community

Imagine a woman at home alone with her young children
late in the afternoon.

Imagine a woman standing on swollen feet, slicing a rye
bread behind the counter at the corner bakery.

Imagine a woman, surrounded by books, studying for
exams, uncertain about her future.

Imagine a woman rushing through her closing argument
to the jury so she can get home in time to fix dinner.

Imagine a woman sitting in silence because no one listens to
the ordinary details of her life.

Imagine this woman . . .

When women feel isolated, tired, confused, harried and
lonely, we turn to other women. We reach out across
kitchen tables, in college dorm rooms, in the "Ladies'
Room" at work. We share hugs and tears and giggles, and
the silences that offer comfort. This is what women have
always done. For some women who have reached out, the
response has been lack of understanding, competition, and
even betrayal. For others the friendships they found have
provided the support and nurturing they needed.

Our grandmothers and great-grandmothers, new immigrants in a strange land, emerged from their isolation and banded together to meet their own needs and the needs of others. They created sisterhoods and women's organizations such as B'nai Brith Women, Hadassah, O.R.T. and the National Council of Jewish Women. In doing this they not only connected with other women, but they also used their talents to grow in new ways.

Many of their daughters who moved out of the cities were like immigrants to suburban society. They too found comfort and connection in these familiar organizations. But for others this was no longer enough. During World War II women had taken on new roles and had seen themselves as contributing to national survival and the survival of the Jewish people. After the war, when they tried to go back to the way things had been, many of them felt frustrated by the constraints of their old roles.

The women's movement as we know it now began with these women, both Jewish and non-Jewish, and with their daughters. These were the women who asked questions: What does it mean to be a woman? To be a mother? To be a daughter? They invented language: "sexism", "female oppression", "consciousness-raising". They formed groups, published books and magazines and created women's studies programs. They challenged existing assumptions about women at home, women in the workplace, women in politics, women in partnership and women in power. They revised history.

Today, as Jewish women, we are still revising our history. We are the immigrants to a new time where there are no road maps and few signposts to guide us. The old roles, the old organizations and even the old language may not meet our needs. By looking at our own lives and the influences upon us, we begin to ask questions: What does it mean to be a Jewish woman? A mother? A daughter? And with our answers we change the shape of the future.

*Opening exercise: Can you remember a moment when you were with another woman or other women and you felt connected? Where were you? Who were you with? What were you doing?*

1. When you were a child who were the women in your family? What were the occasions when they got together? What did they do together?

2. Which women in your family did you feel most connected to? What was it about these women that made your relationships special?

3. Do you remember seeing your mother with other women? What did they do together? Was there a difference in how she related to Jewish and non-Jewish women? What did you learn about women's friendships from observing your mother with her friends?

4. Did you have girl friends when you were growing up? Were you part of a group of girls? Were they Jewish? All of them? Some of them? What did you do together? What was it about the group that felt good? What was it about the group that felt difficult? What did you learn about women's friendships from this group?

5. Was there a girl who was your "best friend?" Was she Jewish? What was special about your friendship? e.g. confiding in each other, having fun together, sharing problems, etc. Were there ever difficulties between you? What were they? e.g. one was more popular, competition between you, talking behind your back, etc. Are you still in touch with her? What did you learn about women's friendships from this experience?

6. What qualities do you now look for in a woman friend? In a male friend? What qualities in a woman prevent you from being her friend? What qualities in a man prevent you from being friends? Do you have different expectations of your men and women friends?

7. Is it important to you that your friends share your be-

liefs, values and/or practices regarding Judaism, women's issues, abortion, political issues, use of drugs and alcohol, smoking, sexual practices, antisemitism, racism? What do you do when there is disagreement? e.g. avoid the subject, talk it out, tolerate the difference, break off the friendship?

8. Thinking about your closest women friend(s) now, what kinds of things do you do together? What is special about your friendship(s)? Are there any difficulties between you? What are they?

9. What do you do in order to maintain your friendship(s) with close women friends? What gets in the way?

10. Has there been an exceptional woman in your life who has supported, encouraged or guided you? Who was she? What did she teach you? What did you learn about women's relationships from this experience? Is there someone you are passing this on to? Who?

11. Do you belong to any women's groups or organizations now? What is it about these groups that feels good to you? What is it that feels difficult? Why did you join these groups? What do you hope to get from them? What do you do for these groups? What do they expect from you?

12. How do you feel when you are the only Jewish person in a group? When you are in a group where Jews are in a minority? In a group that is all Jewish? Do you act differently? How?

13. In your women's groups how do you feel as a Jew? Are Jewish women visible and acknowledged?

—Are there specific programs for and\or about Jewish women?
—Are Jewish women brought in to speak or teach? When they are, are they recognized as Jewish? e.g. Betty Friedan, Bella Abzug, etc.
—Are the Jewish women who are involved in planning or doing programs open about their Judaism?

65

—Are Jewish holidays and Sabbath taken into account when planning programs or other activities?

14. Do you belong to any groups or organizations with men and women members? Do you act differently in these groups than in a group for women only? How? Do you act differently when you are the only woman? How? Do you have different expectations from these groups than from women's groups? What are they?

15. Have your attitudes about women changed in recent years? How? Describe the change in your attitude. e.g. about women at home\at work, women in important leadership roles, women being sexually harassed, etc. Do you think the women's movement has affected your attitude about women's issues? How?

16. Have the activities or programs of your organization(s) changed in recent years because of the women's movement? How? Describe these changes. e.g. speakers on women's issues, participating in marches and rallies, lobbying elected officials, etc. How do you feel about these changes in your organization(s)? Are there any issues or other changes you would like to see addressed? What are they?

*Closing exercise: Read aloud the passage "Imagine a Woman" at the beginning of this chapter. What kind of women were omitted? Complete for yourself the line "Imagine a woman . . ."*

# Jewish Education, Formal and Informal

## Family, programs, teachers and schools

Rabbi Eliezer ben Hyrcanus said that it is better to burn the Torah than to teach it to your daughter. Although many sages disagreed with him, for centuries Jewish women have been denied the Jewish education that their brothers automatically received. A few women learned Hebrew and Torah when there were no sons in the house, when the father was a scholar and teacher (i.e. Rashi), when the family business was printing, or if the daughter was considered unmarriageable. As recently as this century most Jewish women could not read a prayer book in Hebrew or participate in the service in any way. The first recorded *Bat Mitzvah* (Judith Kaplan in 1922) paved the way for more widespread Hebrew and religious education for girls.

*Opening exercise: Can you remember a person from your childhood who was a strong influence on your Jewish education. Who was it? e.g. a parent, grandparent, other family member, friend, teacher, rabbi, etc. How did they influence you?*

1. Can you remember how you learned about Judaism in your family? e.g. family rituals, holiday celebrations, din-

ner table discussions, stories, rites of passage and/or life cycle events.

2. Can you remember how you learned about Judaism in your community? e.g. holiday celebrations, peer involvement in Jewish life, other.

3. When you were a young girl, did you want to go to religious school, Hebrew school or Yeshiva? What kind of Jewish education did other people in your family receive? e.g. parents, grandparents, siblings. What factors were influential? e.g. financial, opportunity, gender, personal motives, etc. What about your friends? How did you feel about this as a child?

4. If you had a formal Jewish education, can you describe the setting in which it took place? Were all the children in your family educated in the same way? If there were differences, what were they? How did that make you feel?

5. Who were your teachers? Were they American or Israeli or other? Were they men or women? Were they more women or men? Do you know if they were trained as teachers? Were they creative around learning? Who was in charge of the school? e.g. rabbi, teacher, principal or other? Was it a man or a woman?

6. Did being a girl raise any particular problems? Were you encouraged to achieve in the same manner as the boys? How long did you attend? Would you have liked to go further? Less? Did being a girl influence how long you attended?

7. Based on your own experiences, what choice did or would you have for your own children regarding a formal Jewish education? Would\did you give the same education to a son or daughter? Would\did you send her\him to a one-day-a week school? an afternoon school? a day school?

8. Are you aware of opportunities for adult Jewish education in your community? What are they? What do you participate in? lectures, programs, rituals, seminars, havurot, etc?

9. In your Jewish community are there specific programs for women, or programs with subject content about women? e.g. women's studies, women's history, women in the Bible, new rituals for women, etc. What are they? If you have participated in any of these what was it like? What impact did it make on your life, your thinking, your attitude, your identity as a Jewish woman?

10. In your personal experience have you been moved as a woman by a series, lecture, workshop or conference? Tell us about it.

11. In your Jewish community are women and men represented equally as speakers and on panels? If so how? If not, how? When women are included, are they invited to address subjects of general interest or only what are considered to be traditional women's topics? What subjects have women spoken about or taught?

12. As an adult looking back, how do you now feel about your Jewish education?

*Closing exercise: If you could plan a one-day program for your particular community (synagogue, women's club, Hillel, etc.) what subject(s) would you want to study?*

# 3

# Jewish Women and College

How we got there or why we didn't;
what it was like.

Before 1940 we rarely heard of a Jewish woman who went to college. Many women did not even have the opportunity to complete high school. At the end of World War II higher education became a real option for both Jewish men and women; but it was not an option if your parents did not believe that a woman needed to be college-educated, and it was not an option if your family could not afford to pay the tuition. For those young women who did go to college, it was their first opportunity to be Jewish in unfamiliar surroundings. We will examine what it was like to go to college (or not), to live among strangers and to decide whether or not to be connected to our Jewish heritage.

*Opening Exercise: Remembering when you were in high school, what was your image of college life?*

1. Who was the first person in your family to go to college. Where and when did they go? What did they study? Who was the first *woman* in your family to go to college? Where and when did she go? What did she study? Did either or both of your parents go to college?

2. What role did your parents play in your decision to go or not to go to college? What were their considrations about

your living at home or away? i.e. money, separation, tradition, geography, gender.

3. What were the expectations of your friends and peers about going to college? What were the expectations of teachers and counselors in your school about going to college? Who encouraged or discouraged you?

4. What was *your* decision? What led to this choice? e.g. money, grades, your friends' choices, reputation and\or curriculum of school, the Jewish presence on campus.

5. How did being Jewish and a woman influence your choice?

The following questions are appropriate only for women who attended college.

6. Tell us about your campus in terms of the following:

—the size and ethnic make-up of the student body
—the geographic location
—the ratio of women to men
—the ratio of Jews to non-Jews
—the ratio of residential students to commuters

7. Where do\did you live? Who do\did you share your living space with? How did this come about? What are\were your feelings about this arrangement? Is\was being Jewish an issue?

8. What groups are\were you a part of? e.g. social, study, organizations and clubs, etc. What is\was the make-up of these groups in terms of gender?

9. What are\were the Jewish organizations on your campus? How are\were you connected to these groups? Are they an active presence? How do you feel about their visibility through posters, events, discussions, newspaper articles and publicity?

10. When are\were you aware of being Jewish in your

classes? What subject matter made you uncomfortable as a Jew? How do\did you respond? Did it matter if the teacher was Jewish? Did it matter if there were other Jewish students in the class? Are\were books written by Jewish authors included in any of your courses? Are\were events in Jewish history included in history, political science, etc.?

11. What events or incidents on your campus made you conscious of being Jewish? What was your response? Has anything abusive or threatening happened to you because you are Jewish?

12. What are\were the womens' organizations on campus? i.e. academic, feminist, service, social. Are\were they an active presence? How are\were you connected to these groups? Do\did you feel comfortable being openly Jewish in these groups?

13. How are\were you aware of being a woman in your classes? What issues do\did you feel comfortable or uncomfortable addressing as a woman? Has\did anything abusive or threatening happened to you because you are a woman? What?

14. Is\was there a Womans' Studies program on campus? Is\was there a Jewish Studies program? Which of these classes have you attended?

*Closing exercise: Reflecting on this discussion, what advice would you give a young woman in high school thinking about going to college?*

# 4

# The Jewish Community

Synagogue and organizations; religious, secular
and political; social and recreational

Before the 19th century, European Jews lived confined to
ghettoes in the Jewish quarter or in the Pale of Settlement.
All Jews were Jews—they had no other options. Even when
they were allowed to become citizens of the country, most
Jews remained in place, although some were able to attend
universities and *gymnasia* and join mainstream society.
When they went to the U.S. and Canada where assimilation
was possible, they had a need to create organizations to
establish and maintain Jewish ties. For some of our parents
and grandparents these organizations were the core of
their lives; others, in their attempts to be more "American",
turned away from these groups. We, too, can make the
choice of belonging to or being outside of the Jewish community.

*Opening exercise: Can you remember and describe a time
when you felt as though you belonged or were a member of
the Jewish community?:*

1. When you were growing up, what Jewish organization
did your parents and grandparents belong to? How did they
participate?

2. In what Jewish activities and\or organizations were you involved during your childhood and young adult years?

3. Based on these early experiences how did you feel about being a part of the organized Jewish community?

4. Do you feel that membership in a Jewish institution or organization defines who belongs to the Jewish community? In your life now, how do you define "Jewish community"?

5. What formal Jewish organizations, if any, do you belong to now? e.g. synagogue, Jewish center, Hillel, fund-raising organizations, membership organization such as National Council of Jewish Women and B'nai Brith, social, political, religious, educational, etc. What do *you* do in these organizations? If you do not belong to a Jewish organization how are you connected to the Jewish community?

*Note: Questions 6 through 9 are for those women who are members of Jewish organizations.*

6. Thinking of the organizations in which you are most involved, what success and satisfaction have you experienced? What kinds of conflicts\issues have you experienced? What did you do about it?

7. Thinking of the organization in which you are most involved, how do people get to be leaders? What obstacles or barriers do you perceive that prevent people from becoming leaders? e.g. being a woman, money, class, occupation, being a convert, etc.

8. In this organization on what basis are people chosen to be recognized and\or honored? Have you ever received such an honor? What was it? Have you or someone you know not received such recognition when it was deserved? Describe the incident.

9. How is this organization connected to the larger Jewish community? e.g. your local federation, national organizations and religious institutions. What impact does your

organization have on this larger community? Are there differences in power between women's organizations and those that include men? How well does this organization reflect your point of view on important issues?

10. Who speaks for *you* within the Jewish community? e.g. what organization, periodical or individual? Who represents your point of view to the non-Jewish community? How do you feel when someone with whom you disagree speaks for the Jewish community? What do you do about it?

11. Have you ever considered working professionally for the organized Jewish community? In what capacity? What benefits would there be in working within the Jewish community? What difficulties do you perceive? e.g. advancement, salary, training, sexism, etc.

*Closing exercise: Having considered all these questions about your relationship to the organized Jewish community, what elements have provided you with a sense of belonging to the community? What can you do to expand these feelings within your organization, group or personal network?*

# 5

# A Job or a Career

Women at home and women at work

Because Jewish men have always been defined by the work they do, and Jewish women have been defined by the men they marry (or don't), we are often surprised when we learn that an older women we know has had a profession or career. Some of our grandmothers and mothers only worked out of financial necessity; they took a job because they needed income and did not have the luxury of choosing and planning a career. Some of our mothers and grandmothers did not have paying jobs; they stayed at home to take care of their children and to manage the endless round of daily chores. Some of our mothers and grandmothers who might have liked to work for pay did not; taking a job would somehow have sent a message that their husbands could not support them. These were limitations that lasted until W.W. II.

Today we are faced with complex choices and challenges. The old pressures still exist: financial need, creating a family and running a household. But now, as a result of the women's movement, there are more professional and career opportunities open to women. There are also new pressures and expectations: we are judged on whether or not we work for pay and what kind of work we do; we are competing with both men and other women in the workplace; we feel pushed to prove our independence and ambition; we are forced to make choices about when (and if) to have children.

We find ourselves in the unenviable position of still being defined by who we marry (or don't) as well as by the work we do (or don't).

In the next two sections we will explore our choices and how we make them, and the meaning of work in our lives.

*Opening Exercise: You are a girl in grade school talking with your friends about what you want to be when you grow up. What is it that you want to be? Why?*

1. Did you tell anyone in your family about this ambition? What was their response?

2. Which women in your family held jobs they were paid for and what did they do? Which women in your family did volunteer work and what was it? How did the women feel about what they did? How did the other family members feel about what the women did?

3. Among your friends and neighbors what did *most* women do: work at home, work for pay, volunteer, etc? In your memory of that time is there one woman who stands out as doing something unusual? Who was she and what did she do?

4. At this early time in your life what jobs did you see women doing in your community? e.g. in school, synagogue, business, etc.

5. When you were in high school what did you say you wanted to be? Was it the same or different from your earlier answer? How? What caused the change?

6. What were your family's expectations for you? What messages did you get about men's work and women's work? About appropriate work for Jews and non-Jews? About class and status?

7. What messages did you get outside your family? How did they influence your ideas of who you wanted to be and what you wanted to do? Was there some person who supported and encouraged your aspirations?

8. Did you choose to go to college, or get some special training? Why or why not? How did this relate to who you wanted to be? To what you wanted to do?

9. What are you doing now? What were the circumstances, both accidental and planned, that brought you to this place in your life? e.g. your family encouraged\discouraged you, your partner encouraged\discouraged you, family crisis, an unexpected opportunity arose etc. How do you feel about what you do?

10. What compromises and negotiations did you make about work? e.g. delayed marriage, career or having children, conflict with partner's career, not wanting to relocate, salary and benefit considerations etc.

*Closing exercise: What do you see yourself doing a year from now? What stands in your way? What is the first step you can take to move toward that goal?*

# 6

# The Places We Work

## Responding to our working environment

*Opening exercise: What was your first job? Where? What did you like best about this job? What did you not like? What did you learn about work from this job?*

1. Using the following list of categories as a suggestion, how would you describe yourself at this time in your life:

  —Student, full or part time
  —Employed, full or part time
  —Seeking training or "experience"
  —Self-employed, work at home
  —Self-employed, work outside the home
  —Homemaker, full or part time.
  —Looking for a job, full or part time
  —Re-entering the job market
  —Volunteer, full or part time
  —Unable to work

What is it about being in this category that you like? What is it that you don't like?

2. Where do you work or volunteer now? What work do you do? Paid or unpaid? Do you get benefits? Why do you work or volunteer?

3. Are there other women at the place you work or volunteer? What is the proportion of women to men? Is your supervisor or boss a woman or man? What is the highest position held by a woman? Do you think that women are treated different from men? How do you feel as a woman in your work or volunteer organization?

4. Are there other Jews working or volunteering with you? Are they men or women? What is the proportion of Jews to non-Jews? Is your supervisor or boss Jewish? What is the highest position held by a Jew? By a Jewish woman? Do you think that Jews are treated different from non-Jews? How do you feel as a Jewish woman at your work or in your volunteer organization?

5. Have you ever had a conflict at your work or volunteer organization between your Jewish values and\or observance and what was expected or required of you? What was the conflict? How was it resolved?

6. If you work or volunteer for a Jewish communal service organization, or for a Jewish owned company, are Jewish values expressed in the work place? What are they? How are they expressed?

7. How does your Jewish community support working women and women who volunteer their time? e.g. child care, after school activities, transportation, career training, job placement, etc.

8. Can you describe your working conditions with regard to the following:

—Expectation of appearance (age, weight, style of dress, make-up, hairstyle)
—Your ability to express complaints and the response to them (heat, light, smoking, salary, hours, etc.)
—Advancement and equal pay for women
—Attitude toward lesbian women
—Attitude toward women with disabilities
—Ongoing training
—Attitude toward union membership

—Unrealistic expectations of your job performance

9. Does the place where you work have a stated family policy? e.g. flexible working hours, parental leave, provision for emergency time off, support for child care, etc. What are your personal needs? Are they being met? How?

10. Who are your friends at work or in your volunteer organizations? Are they women? Men? Jewish? Non-Jewish? Do you have a social relationship with them outside of the workplace? Do these friendships change your work relationships? How?

11. Have you ever had to deal with any of these situations in your employment or volunteer work?

*At your Job:*

Being underpaid
Earning more or less than partner\spouse
Passed over for promotion
Being afraid to apply for promotion
Little or no opportunity for advancement
Working at a level below your ability
Working at a job that doesn't use your skills or talents
Working at a job for which you feel inadequate
Not being acknowledged for the work you do
Not being satisfied with your own job performance
Feeling that your work does not make a difference
Being harassed, sexually, verbally or physically
Not having enough time to meet your own performance
    standards
Being offered a job transfer or travel opportunity
Partner\spouse being offered transfer or travel opportunity that conflicts with your work
Balancing demands of extra work with personal needs
    and family expectations
Having to take a leave to care for parent, partner, child
    or self

Not reimbursed for money you personally spend on organization activities (meals, travel, phone calls, postage, etc.)

Having higher status or title than partner\spouse

Not getting position or office you qualify for and expect

Being afraid to question the status quo or authority of the organization

Little or no opportunity for advancement

Not working at a level for which you are qualified

Being forced into a position in which you are uncomfortable or not qualified

Not being acknowledged

Not being able to complete work because of organizational bureaucracy

Feeling that you don't make a difference

Being harassed, sexually, verbally or physically

Balancing demands of volunteer position with family expectations

What did you do about that situation? (If you have not personally faced any of these situations, which concern you the most?)

*Closing exercise: Given your present work or volunteer situation, what is most satisfying to you? If you could change anything to make work or volunteering better, what would it be?*

# 7

# Authority and Control

## How we feel about power

"Power" . . . "Authority" . . . "Control" . . . When used to describe ourselves or other women, the very words make us squirm. They conjure up images of a tough, bitchy, deep-voiced, insensitive woman who is incapable of loving or being loved. While all of us share this discomfort, as Jewish women we have the added fear of being labelled as a pushy, Jewish shrew. This fear is not without cause.

In our culture, power has traditionally been considered a masculine trait, leaving femininity to be equated with powerlessness. The dilemma for us has been how to exert power, authority and control while remaining the caring, warm women we want to be. And yet, the dictionary tells us that "power" is the ability to do something or anything; that "authority" is an influence that creates respect and confidence; and "control" is to check, regulate and keep within limits. None of these definitions implies either masculinity or femininity.

Although Judaism is a patriarchal religion, we have ancient examples of women who exercised power, authority and control: Miriam the prophet, Queen Esther who acted to save her people, Deborah the judge who led the Jews in battle, and Judith the young widow who bravely slew Holofernes and routed his troops. Down through the ages the stories of exceptional Jewish women have been "written out of history."* These women existed, they acted, but they were lost to us as models until recent feminist scholars rediscovered and reclaimed them.

Throughout history, the Jewish values of modesty and humility have inhibited women from taking seriously their own power and authority. Within our own lifetime *we* are still confined by narrowly defined sex roles. When we exert power or authority we risk being ridiculed, diminished and dismissed. When we realize how powerless we are, we feel frustrated, enraged and depressed. It is only by raising our consciousness—talking to each other woman-to-woman, recognizing our common experience, and naming our struggle—that we can move beyond isolation into the full expression of ourselves as powerful women.

*Opening exercise: Our dictionary definition of power is "the ability to do something or anything." How would you define the word "power"? Who would you say has power?*

1. When you were a child who did you see as the "boss" in your family? What did s\he do that made you feel that s\he was the boss? How did s\he show her\his power? How did that make you feel? How did other family members respond?

2. Who else in your family ever acted as "boss"? When? In what situations? What did s\he do?

3. As a child in your family what did you do to try to get your feelings heard? e.g. said what was necessary, expressed your needs, behaved extra good, whined, threw a temper tantrum, etc. How did your family respond to this? e.g. they listened to you and believed you, they ignored you, they ridiculed you, they called you names, they punished you, etc. How did this make you feel? Was there a person in your family who you felt was particularly respectful of

*Sondra Henry & Emily Taitz, *Written Out of History: Our Jewish Foremothers,* New York: Biblio Press, 1990.

your feelings? Who was this person and what did this mean to you?

4. When you were in school how did you respond to your teachers, principals or others in authority? e.g. obedient and respectful, defiant, rebellious, scared, class clown, etc. Can you remember an incident that reflected this behavior?

5. When you were an adolescent was there an "in-group" at your school? Were you part of that group? Were you part of any group? What power did this in-group have over other people in the school? e.g. getting elected to offices, being cheerleaders, deciding who would be invited to parties, etc. What power did your group have over you? e.g. what you wore, who you talked to, what parties you went to, etc.

6. When was the first time that you felt you were "really grown-up"?

| | |
|---|---|
| —Left home | —Came out |
| —Moved into own place | —Started college |
| —Became self-supporting | —Finished college |
| —Involved in committed relationship | —Worked full-time |
| | —Had a child |
| —Got married | —Other |

What was it about this change that made you feel different? Did people treat you differently? How? In what ways did you feel you had more control over your life?

7. Our dictionary definition of authority is "an influence that creates respect and confidence". How would *you* define authority? Who would *you* say has authority?

8. In your life now who has authority over you? What is this relationship like and how does it make you feel? How do people you perceive to be in positions of authority make you feel? e.g. police, I.R.S., doctors, rabbis, therapists, lawyers, professors, older relatives, etc. How do you react to these people when you have to deal with them?

9. In your life now, over whom do you have authority? What is this relationship like and how does it make you feel? How do you feel about saying "No", setting limits, giving instructions or orders to other people? e.g. waiter or waitress, housekeeper, cab driver, hairdresser, physician, attorney, plumber, etc. How do you react when you have to deal with them?

10. How do you feel about saying "No", setting limits, giving directions to people close to you? e.g. spouse, partner, roomate, parent, child, friend, etc. How do you feel when your communication is defied or ignored? What is your response? e.g. try again, sulk, cry, scream, etc.

11. How do you feel when someone close to you says "No", sets limits or gives directions to you? How do you respond?

12. From the list below, which have made you feel more powerful? Can you describe an incident which would show this feeling? From this list which have made you feel less powerful? Can you describe an incident which would show this feeling?

| | |
|---|---|
| —Being a woman | —Being a Jew |
| —Being a student | —Being single\married |
| —Being a lesbian or bisexual | —Being divorced |
| | —Having a disability |
| —Being a widow | —Reentering workplace |
| —Working\retired | |

—Looking a certain way (thin\fat, short\tall, pretty, etc)

| | |
|---|---|
| —Being young\old | —Being a woman in a synagogue |

—Speaking before a mixed audience

13. Our dictionary definition of control is "to check, regulate and keep within limits". How would *you* define control? Who would *you* say has control?

14. Are there any areas in your life where you would like to have more control? What are they? Are there areas in your

life where you would like to give up some control? What are they?

*Closing exercise: Reflecting back to the opening of this chapter, complete the following statement: A Jewish woman doesn't have to be tough, insensitive and pushy to be powerful. I am powerful when I . . .*

# 8

# The Media Mirror

How Jewish women are portrayed in movies and
television

Mirrors reflect back to us a representation of who we
are—our size, coloring, our dress, the way we comb our
hair. But this representation is only a two dimensional
picture of our physical self.

It doesn't show how we think, what we feel, the daily
kindnesses or cruelties we encounter.

It doesn't show the contributions we make to the lives of
others.

It doesn't show our histories as Jewish women.

In our culture, the mass media—films, books, television,
comedians,—mirror a version of ourselves which is two-
dimensional, and lacking the contours and textures of our
real lives. As Jewish women we see ourselves continually
portrayed as stereotypes, rather than as the complex people
we are.

The birth of filmaking at the beginning of the 20th century coincided with mass Jewish immigration from Eastern Europe, but the early pioneer Jewish filmakers,
uncomfortable with their immigrant roots, ignored the
profound Jewish issues of their day: the rise of Nazism,
antisemitism, the Holocaust, and the creation of the state of

Israel. For decades what was portrayed was an Americanized Jewish male.

For women, the stereotype was the Jewish mother, whose on-screen life reached a new stature with a film of her own in 1951. *Molly* (Goldberg) is an asexual dumpling of a woman who never gets angry. Her whole life revolves around her husband and children and gossiping with her neighbors. Though she is presented as dignified and self-sacrificing, she is basically a comic caricature of a Jewish immigrant woman. At the end of this same decade, a new cinematic caricature of a Jewish woman made her appearance in *Marjorie Morningstar* (1958). Marjorie represents a different image: young, attractive, upper-middle class, well-dressed, and thoroughly Americanized. She is also spoiled, self-absorbed, sexual, empty in spite of a good education,—a Princess who symbolizes her father's success.

In the following decades, variations of these two characters, the Jewish Mother and the Jewish Princess, as well as the crass, flamboyant, outspoken woman who is often a target for ridicule, and the abrasive, intellectual, have become screen cliches.* As Jewish women, we have watched these movies. We have left the theatre or turned off the television, filled with the larger-than-life images presented to us. Sometimes we have been accepting and felt entertained. Sometimes we have been angry at the embarrassing stereotypes we have seen. And though we now frequently see ourselves reflected in the mirror that films, television and comedians provide, what we see is still usually a distortion; what we still don't hear often enough are the voices of Jewish women telling the truth about their own personal struggles.

In this section we will examine in depth the two most

*See for example *Goodbye Columbus, Where's Poppa, Portnoy's Complaint, Private Benjamin, Down and Out in Beverly Hills, Ruthless People, Dirty Dancing, New York Stories, Crossing Delancey, White Palace, The Way We Were, Yentl, For the Boys, Heartbreak Kid.*
On television see *Rhoda, thirtysomething, Brooklyn Bridge.*

prevalent exaggerations of the Jewish woman in film and television, so that we can consciously break through the ongoing portrayal of Jewish women in a negative light. As we become more aware and refuse to accept these images, we can educate our families and friends and support the work of those filmmakers who show us real Jewish women.

*Opening exercise: Can you think of a film or television program you've seen recently which featured a Jewish woman character? How was this character presented? How did you feel about her?*

1. When you were a child, did you see any films or TV programs with Jewish women characters? What do you remember about these characters? How did you feel about them? Were they like any women in your family? Who?

2. As a teenager, what did you learn from TV and the movies about what it meant to be a Jewish woman, e.g. what to wear/what not to wear; how to behave/how not to behave? Do you remember any specific films or programs that taught you these lessons?

3. At the present time, what are the words and images you would use to describe a *Jewish Mother?* What does she look like? How does she talk? How does she dress? Where does she shop? What does she do with her time? What does she value most? What else can you say about her? What do you admire about her? What do you dislike about her?

4. Which of these same words and images of a *Jewish Mother* would you use to describe women in your own family? Which would describe other Jewish women you know? Could any of these words and images apply to a woman who isn't Jewish? Which of these words and images would you consider to be a stereotype? From where did you get these words and images?

5. Can you remember seeing a film or tv program in which a stereotype of a *Jewish Mother* appeared? Which film or program? Which image(s) of the *Jewish Mother* was pre-

sented? How did the other characters in the story respond to her? Was the story told from her point of view? If not, from whose point of view was it told?

6. With regard to this same film or program, how did you feel about this *Jewish Mother?* What did you like about her? What did you dislike about her? Did she remind you of someone you know personally? Who?

7. At the present time, what are the words and images you would use to describe a *Jewish Princess?* What does she look like? How does she talk? How does she dress? Where does she shop? What does she do with her time? What does she value most? What else can you say about her? What do you admire about her? What do you dislike about her?

8. Which of these same words and images describing a *Jewish Princess* would you use to describe women in your own family? Which would describe other Jewish women you know? Could any of these words and images apply to a woman who isn't Jewish? Which of these words and images would you consider to be a stereotype? From where did you get these words and images?

9. Can you remember seeing a film or tv program in which a stereotype of a *Jewish Princess* appeared? Which film or program? Which image(s) of the *Jewish Princess* was presented? How did the other characters in the story respond to her? Was the story told from her point of view? If not, from whose point of view was it told?

10. With regard to this same film or program, how did you feel about this *Jewish Princess?* What did you like about her? What did you dislike about her? Did she remind you of someone you know personally? Who?

11. Have you ever been called a *Jewish Mother,* a *Jewish Princess,* or a *JAP (Jewish American Princess)?* What were the circumstances? How did you feel? How did you respond? Which of the words and images you have used to describe a *Jewish Mother* and a *Jewish Princess* would *you* use to describe yourself?

12. Outside of these stereotypes of the Jewish Mother and the Jewish Princess, can you think of other ways in which Jewish women have been commonly portrayed in films and on TV? What characteristics have filmmakers used to indicate "Jewishness"?

13. Can you remember a film or program in which a Jewish woman was portrayed in a positive manner? Which movie or program? Which character? What was it about this character that you saw as positive? e.g. her courage or aggressiveness, her intellect, her independence, her warmth, etc. Do you know if the actress playing this character was Jewish?

14. When Jewish women produce or direct films (Bette Midler—*For the Boys,* Barbra Streisand—*Yentl, Prince of Tides*), do you think that they portray Jewish women in a different way? How are they different?

*Closing exercise: If you were given the power to create a film or program to tell the story of a Jewish woman you know or have known, whose story would you tell? What is it about this woman that you'd want your audience to know? What is it about her life you'd want to convey? What makes it a Jewish story?*

ACTIVITY

Having examined the stereotype of the Jewish Mother and the Jewish Princess, we would like to expand our ability to look at all portrayals of Jewish women in our mass culture: books, magazines, newspapers, advertisements, comedians, theater, film, and television. We want to consider the following whenever we see a Jewish woman portrayed:

Is she created by a man or a woman?
What is her appearance?
What are her particular mannerisms?
How does she speak?
Does she belittle or make fun of herself?
Is she dependent or independent?
    aggressive or passive?

straightforward or manipulative?

thrifty or extravagant?

How is she shown relating to her parents and family?

Her partner/spouse? Her children? Her friends?

How is her Jewish life shown? Religious practice?

Political involvement? Organizations?

How is her Jewish heritage described?

What positive qualities do we see in her?

What negative qualities?

Is she portrayed sympathetically?

Whose point of view is represented in her portrayal?

Is she held up for comparison with a nonJewish woman?

# 9

# God, Prayer, and Spirituality

## Personal beliefs and practice

As Jewish women we have much in common: we are all women, and we all share a heritage and a tradition. And yet, because of the diversity of Jewish life, we express our connection to that heritage in many different ways.

For some women, almost every act of daily life is immersed in the traditional practices of family purity and keeping a kosher home.

For some women, High Holidays and the family seder are the times for affirming their Jewish connection.

For some women, their connection to Judaism is only now being awakened.

For some women, their connection to the tradition is to redefine it, as they redefine women's roles in Judaism.

The way we connect with our tradition may be a continuation or expansion of the practices we learned in our families, or it may be a break with our past:

a woman from a secular non-religious home lights Sabbath candles;

a child returns from summer camp and teaches her parents new melodies to old prayers;

a mother of two becomes a rabbi;

a college student and her mother study together to become *b'not mitzvah;*

a grandmother is called to the Torah for the first time;
a group of women study Talmud and ask new questions.

But whatever forms our connections have taken, as Jewish women we have had to face these painful questions: "How can there be a God who let six million die? How can there be a God who lets children suffer?" Our answers are as varied as our personal practices.

For some of us, God's ways are unknowable and God is beyond our comprehension; our response is acceptance.

For some of us the questions are too painful even to think about.

For some of us, there can be no God who would let such injustice happen; our response is rejection of belief.

For some of us, the response is not clear; we can only continue to ask the questions.

*Opening exercise: Can you remember a Jewish occasion or ritual from your childhood that felt special to you, a time when everything felt right? What was it about that moment that felt spiritual? Can you describe an occasion or ritual that was not Jewish that felt spiritual or holy?*

1. When you were a child, did your family have any Jewish traditions or practices? Which were your favorites? Why? If your family didn't have any such traditions, how did you feel about this?

2. Did your family say any blessings or prayers? e.g. bedtime prayers, blessings at meals, etc. Did you have a special prayer that you said to yourself privately? Where and when?

3. Were there times in your childhood when you felt excluded from or uncomfortable with Jewish traditions? What were they? Did you ever talk about your feelings? To whom? What was their response?

4. Did your family belong to a synagogue when you were a

child? Did you ever attend religious services? On what occasions? What was your experience of attending services?

5. Did you have a personal childhood image of God? Describe how you imagined God at that time, e.g. creator, protector, judge, father, mother, spirit, healer, etc.

6. When you were 12 or 13 did you have a *bat mitzvah?* What did it mean to you personally? Did you have a confirmation? What did it mean to you personally?

7. When you were in high school, were you connected to religious life? e.g. synagogue, camp, organizations, family observances. How? Can you remember an experience or occasion from that time that felt special or spiritual?

8. Can you remember a Jewish occasion or ritual from your adult life that felt special to you, a time when everything felt right? What was it about that moment that felt spiritual? Can you describe an occasion or ritual that was not Jewish that felt spiritual or holy?

9. When was the first time you decided to join a Jewish community independent of your parents or family? e.g. college or earlier, after college, when you got into a committed relationship or married, when your children were born, etc. What made you join the community? e.g. looking for community, brought in by someone, for spouse/partner, for children, etc.

10. Do you belong to a synagogue now? When do you attend religious services? What is your experience of attending services? Does the language of prayer, Hebrew or English, make a difference? Have you ever wanted to study Hebrew? Have you ever participated in leading a service?

11. In your synagogue, do women read from the Torah? Say blessings for the Torah reading? Are counted in the *minyan* (quorum of 10 people for prayer)? Lead parts of the service? Wear *tallit* (prayer shawl) or *kipot* (yarmulke)? Are the matriarchs (Sarah, Rebekah, Rachel, and Leah) included in prayers that refer to the patriarchs (Abraham, Isaac, and Jacob)? Have you attended a service led by a

woman rabbi and/or cantor? Are these changes different from your earlier experiences? How do you feel about these changes?

12. Do you have any personal images of God at this time? Describe how you imagine God, e.g. creator, protector, judge, father, mother, spirit, healer, partner, lover, etc.

13. What images or feelings do you experience when we read this version of the Kiddush?

> *Blessed is the Lord our God, King of the Universe, Creator of the fruit of the vine,*

What images or feelings do you experience when we read this version of the Kiddush by Marcia Falk?*

> *Let us bless the source of life that ripens fruit on the vine as we weave the branches of our lives into the tradition.*

14. Historically, Judaism has referred to the presence of God as the *Shekhinah,* which many understand to mean the feminine aspects of God. Is this image familiar to you? Where have you used it? Describe how you imagine the *Shekhinah.* Some women are now using the English word *Goddess* in their prayers and blessings. Have you heard any Jewish prayers referring to the Goddess? How do you feel about this new language?

15. In your life today, which of the following are the most spiritually satisfying for you? Which are the least satisfying:

—welcoming the Sabbath
—attending religious services
—participating in Bible or Torah study

*Marcia Lee Falk, Copyright ©, *The Book of Blessings: A Feminist Jewish Reconstruction of Prayer,* Harper/San Francisco, forthcoming.

—attending a Jewish summer camp
—participating in a life-cycle event (*bar* or *bat mitzvah,*
baby naming or *brit milah,* wedding, etc.)
—going to the *mikvah* (ritual bath)
—participating in a *havurah*
—participating in a *Rosh Chodesh* group
—attending a Jewish women's program or class
—attending a feminist seder
—attending a spiritual retreat
—attending a Gay/Lesbian synagogue
—creating new services and/or rituals. . . .
—any other

16. From the following list, have there been any events in your life that you would like to have acknowledged with a ritual?

—your first period
—leaving home for college
—menopause
—the moment of giving birth
—becoming a grandmother
—divorce or ending a relationship
—breast-feeding or weaning a child

—adoption of a child
—coming out as a lesbian or bisexual
—miscarriage or abortion
—your daughter's first period
—your youngest child leaving home
—*Simchat Chochma*— Wisdom Ceremony (60th birthday)
—other. . .

*Closing exercise: Choose one event, moment, or special time in your life now that you would like to acknowledge. On a card or piece of paper, complete the following: "As a woman, I feel blessed because. . . ." Each of us will read aloud what we have written to create a "New Woman's" collective blessing.*

*III. The Personal Becomes Political*

"If not now, when?"

In our first two sections we have looked at the forces that have shaped us as Jewish women: our families, our communities, our economic class, our religious practice, our education, our relationships, our work. We have tried to understand how the many different messages we have received have influenced our perceptions of ourselves: our bodies, our sexuality, our self-esteem, our dreams, our hopes, our expectations. As we have named our feelings, we have acknowledged our pain and our joy, our achievements and our disappointments; the contradictory nature of our lives. Above all, we have recognized that we are not alone. While we have learned how much we have in common, we have also learned how unique we are.

In these sessions we have paused; we have taken a break from the pressures of our daily lives. By speaking aloud and hearing the voices of other women, we have come to value ourselves and each other in new ways. We see that we do not have to accept other people's ideas about who we are or who we ought to be. We *do* have choices: we can express ourselves; we can assert ourselves; we can create change.

In this concluding section, *The Personal Becomes Political,* we take what we have discovered about our personal lives and look at the political implications. By political we mean "not . . . political parties or voting but . . . the concept of *power* in society: who has it, how it is used, how one gets it, how society is managed."* The purpose of this section, indeed of this entire guide, is to help us see the connections between these issues of power and our personal lives.

Whether we feel safe walking home alone at night, whether we can find out what we need to know about birth control and family planning, whether we can find a place for an elderly Jewish relative to live in safety and comfort, whether we can get to work or school or shopping without a car, whether we are required to work or attend class on the Sabbath or a Jewish holiday—these are only a few examples

*NOW Guidelines for Feminist Consciousness-Raising, Washington, DC, National Organization for Women, 1982.

of situations in which our options are limited by the decisions of government, the courts, corporations, agencies and organizations. As individuals we change our behavior in order to adjust to our circumstances, to do the best we can to get along. But alone we can't change these situations, even though we want to. Our Jewish traditions of *tzedakah* (justice), *tikkun olam* (repairing the world), and *gemilut chasidim* (good deeds) direct us to be involved in improving our world. But it feels overwhelming. There is so much to do. How do we begin?

In these next chapters we will think about some of the larger issues which affect our lives: control of our bodies, antisemitism, Israel, local and national politics. Together we will examine our own attitudes and prejudices, our sources of information, our willingness to challenge authorities and our ability to take action and make a difference. Writing a letter to your legislator urging support for health care, taking food to a synagogue food bank, creating a synagogue policy to include gay or lesbian couples as family members, joining with other women to protest sexual harassment on campus, forming a committee to demand a traffic light so that children may cross safely on their way to school, organizing a community program for women who need to change careers or enter the job market, running for public office—these are only a few examples of actions that *can* make a difference.

In each of our lives there is something that is really important to us, something that we would like to change. The Talmud teaches us that we are not expected to complete the work, but we are expected to begin. Let us begin . . .

# 1

# Control of our Bodies

*Opening exercise: During the course of a month what
changes are you aware of in your body that relate to your
menstrual cycle? e.g. swelling, mood swings, hot flashes,
food cravings, etc. Do these changes affect your life in any
way? How? Do your family or friends react to you differently at these times? How? Has anyone ever labeled your
emotions as being due to PMS or menopause? How did that
make you feel? How did you respond?*

1. Are any of your doctors women? Jewish? Why did you
choose\not choose a woman doctor? A Jewish doctor? If you
had to choose a new doctor would you prefer a man or a
woman? Jewish or non-Jewish?

2. How do you feel about being without clothes in your
doctor's office? How do you feel about being touched by your
doctor or nurse? Have you ever felt that you were being
touched in an intrusive or inappropriate way? Did you say
or do anything? Why or why not?

3. When you go to the doctor, are there questions or concerns about your body that you feel uncomfortable expressing? Why? How does your doctor respond when you do
state your concerns and questions? What do you do when
you don't understand the answer? When you need more
information? When you don't agree with the doctor? When
you want a second opinion?

4. Have you ever asked your doctor about any of the following:

Birth control and family planning
Pregnancy and childbirth
PMS\menstrual problems
Fertility\infertility
Genetic diseases
Sexual problems
Menopause and\or estrogen replacement therapy
Osteoporosis
Hysterectomy
Incontinence
Aging
Abortion
Sexually transmitted disease
AIDS
Depression
Migraine
Sleeping problems
Addiction(s) to alcohol &\or drugs
Eating disorders
Prescription drugs
Back pain
Pain or fatigue of unknown origin
Heart disease
Breast cancer
Lung cancer, and other forms cancer
Diet, nutrition and exercise
Plastic and\or cosmetic surgery

How did the doctor respond? Were you satisfied with the information? Which of these subjects has your doctor brought up? Which of these subjects did your doctor fail to discuss even though it might have been appropriate?

5. Who makes the medical decisions for you? For your

children? For your aged parents? You? Your doctor? Your family? Other? Are you aware of or have you chosen to use alternative medical care? e.g. homeopathy, osteopathy, chiropractery, accupuncture, other?

6. There are many important health issues for women; some of them are listed in question 4. Your group can select any of those issues concerning control of our bodies which are most important to you. To select the issues that your group wants to discuss please refer to the section in the introduction, *Making a Group Decision*. Use the following questions as the basis for your discussion.

What are your personal concerns about this issue?
Have you talked about your concerns with anyone? Who?
Do you feel that you have the information you need about this issue? (prevention, diagnosis, treatment)
Where do you get your information?
If you have conflicting information from different sources, how do you decide whom to believe?
Is this a problem in the Jewish community?
How does your Jewish community deal with this issue?
What do you think should be done to increase women's awareness about this issue?
Are you aware if research is being done on this issue?
Are you aware of any organizations working on this issue? Are any of them Jewish?
Are you involved in such organizations? How?
Do any of the other organizations to which you belong take a position on this issue?
Have you ever personally taken action on this issue? How?
Do you know if care is available for all women who need it, regardless of their income?

7. One out of four girls will experience sexual abuse by the

time they are 18, probably by a family member.* One out of every three women will be a victim of rape in her lifetime.** Nearly 66% of all married women experience physical violence in their marriage.*** 85% of women report being harassed at some time in the workplace.****

Do you think these statistics apply to Jewish women? Why? Why not?

Do you ever think about the possibility of violence in your life?

In what situations are you particularly aware of this? e.g. walking alone at night, being alone in an elevator with a strange man, being alone with a particular family member, etc.

What adjustments do you make in your daily life because of your fear of violence? e.g. have extra locks on doors or windows, know who's at the door before opening, don't put your whole name on mailbox or in the phone book, etc.

What is your response to the myth that women who are raped, harassed or battered "ask for it" by their dress &\or behavior?

What is your response to the myth that "normal Jewish men" don't commit rape, violence or incest?

What is your response to the myth that a sexual harasser doesn't mean any harm, he's just "complimenting" you?

Have there been programs or discussions about these issues in your Jewish community? Women's organization(s)? If not, why not?

Are you aware of organizations working on these issues? Are any of them Jewish?

What do you know about the laws regarding rape, vio-

*Linda Tsherhart Sanford, *Silent Children—a Book for Parents about the Prevention of Child Sexual Abuse,* Garden City, N.Y.: Anchor Press\Doubleday, 1980.
**Los Angeles Commission on Assaults Against Women.
***B'nai Brith Women, *Facts about Domestic Violence,* Washington, D.C., 1991.
****Abbie Liebman, California Women's Law Center, reported in *The Jewish Journal,* Los Angeles, Oct. 18, 1991.

lence, and harassment in your community? e.g. who is required to report an incident, what is required of police, doctor or hospital, what evidence is acceptable, etc.

Where would you tell a woman to go for help? Do you know what resources are available in your community?

What do you think should be done to increase women's awareness of these issues?

Have you ever personally taken action on these issues? How?

*Closing exercise: In reflecting on our conversations in this session is there something that you saw that you would like to change in your life? If so, what is it and how would you begin?*

ACTIVITIES

1. Check your library to see if they have *The New Our Bodies, Ourselves* by the Boston Women's Health Book Collective, or other feminist publications on women's health issues. If there are none, ask the library to purchase some, or donate some of these books.

2. Talk to your doctor about an issue that concerns you.

3. Check library resources (*The Reader's Guide to Periodical Literature,* computer data banks) or your congressional representative's office for more information and current research on an issue that concerns you.

Find out (by use of library reference material) who is providing funds for this research—government agency, pharmaceutical companies, non-profit foundations. If there is no research being done write a letter to your legislator to express your concern.

4. During the coming week, notice advertisements and commercials about women's bodies, birth control, sanitary napkins, tampons, deodorants, diet programs, acne medications, any ads for drugs that focus on women (sleeping medications, laxatives, headache remedies, etc.). Think about what these ads say about women's bodies and normal

functions. How are these ads different from ads for men? What kind of women are portrayed? (their ethnicity, class, age and body type, the setting, their relationships) How do these ads make you feel?

If you find these advertisements or commercials degrading in any way, write to the company and to the newspaper, magazine or television station to register your complaint.

5. What are the laws of your state or province about reproductive choice and the right of women to have an abortion? Find out if all women have equal access to all options. Join a local or national organization whose position you agree with. Write to your legislator to support your position.

6. Learn how to do a self-breast examination and teach it to at least one other woman.

7. Find out if your community has a battered women's shelter &\or a rape crisis center. Find out how many people use the services. How many people are turned away? Where do these agencies get their money? Find out if they get support from the Jewish community. Find out the needs they have for volunteers, funds, clothing, toys. Provide some of these items on your own; ask other people to do the same; organize a drive to collect more of these items.

8. Ask your local United Way and\or Jewish Family Service if your community has programs to re-educate men who are rapists or batterers. If there is such a program, ask to see the materials the men are taught. If there is no such program talk to the director about the possibility of starting one.

9. Develop and send to every student a written policy condemning rape and other sexual assaults, emphasizing that these crimes will not be tolerated on your campus.

10. Find out what your community's response to AIDS has been by contacting your local Public Health Department, United Way, local hospitals and hospices. Find out their needs for volunteers, funds, clothing, toys. Is the Jewish community involved in any of these programs? Provide some of the needed items on your own; ask other people to do the same; organize a drive to collect more of these items.

11. Take it upon yourself to get your organization or school to sponsor a program about one of these important women's issues.

## 2

# Our Marginal Status

### Jews in society: antisemitism and alienation

*Opening exercise: Can you remember the first time you recognized that you were considered different because you were Jewish? What were the circumstances? How did you feel? What did you do?*

1. How did your family talk about non-Jews, other racial groups and ethnic minorities? What names did they use? How did you feel about that? What names do you use now?

2. How did your family talk about Jews? Were there particular Jewish groups that they admired and\or supported? Which ones? Were there groups that they disliked or resented? Which ones? What group(s) did they feel part of?

3. How did you learn about antisemitism in your family? In your Jewish community? Do you remember hearing about pogroms, the Holocaust, the McCarthy period, the Rosenbergs, the U.N. anti-Zionist resolution, white supremacists, Farrakhan and Black antisemitism, anti-Israel points of view? How did this influence your thinking about being Jewish in the world?

4. What stereotypes of Jewish people, beliefs and practice are you aware of? Which if any of these have been attributed to you? Have you or anyone in your family done anything to

be "less Jewish"? e.g. change your name, change your appearance, move, join a particular club or organization, etc.

5. What was your first experience of antisemitism? What did you do? How did you feel? Did you discuss it with anyone? What was the response? Did anything change in your life because of this experience? e.g. end of friendship or relationship, self-conscious about being Jewish, etc.

6. Where and to whom do you tell Jewish jokes? Jokes about women? Jokes about other ethnic minorities? When Jewish jokes or antisemitic remarks are made in your presence, how do you react? In what way is your response different if you are in a Jewish group? A mixed group? A place where you are the only Jew?

7. In what way have you or someone you know been threatened or abused because of being Jewish? Of being a woman? Where did this occur? e.g. on campus, at work, in a community organization, etc. Did this change your sense of what it means to be Jewish in this society? How?

8. Have you ever personally experienced insensitivity to Jews and Jewish practices at your school, workplace or in your community? e.g. dances, exams, football games scheduled on Yom Kippur, ham or shrimp served at an official dinner, invocation at a public event addressed to "Jesus Christ, our Lord", etc. What were the circumstances? What did you do?

9. What is the most recent antisemitic material or incident you have encountered? What was your response? How do you feel when you speak out? When you don't speak out? When another Jewish person speaks out in a confronting way? When someone Jewish says they are speaking for Jews but you don't agree with her\him? When no one speaks out?

10. When you see a Jewish star, a mezuzah, a *chai* or other Jewish symbols in the media, in cartoons or worn as jewelry, how do you feel? What is your reaction when an Israeli flag, a large Chanukah menorah or other Jewish

symbol is displayed in a public place? How do you feel about wearing or displaying these symbols?

11. How do you respond when you hear about an accident in the news? Do you look to see if any Jews were injured? Are you relieved if there are no obvious Jewish names? Do you look to see if there are any Jewish names when your community newspaper announces local honors or awards? Do you notice when Jews are honored nationally or internationally? e.g. Nobel prize, Oscar, Tony., etc. How do you feel when a Jew is charged with a crime? When you disagree with what appears to be the opinion of the majority of Jews? e.g. Jesse Jackson's presidential campaign, the Gulf War, Israeli politics, etc. Do you ever feel that Jews make too much of antisemitic incidents? Too little? Do you expect Jews to behave better than non-Jews? Why?

*Closing exercise: While we cannot change history, how do you think we should pass on this information to future generations? What can you do to transform these feelings of victimization into meaningful action?*

## ACTIVITIES

1. Take a Jewish calendar to your local school district office and local community organizations to inform them about important Jewish holidays. Be aware of events that conflict with Jewish holidays: tests, dances, sports, etc. Also become aware of the content of holiday programs: singing Christmas carols, reciting prayers, etc. Call this to their attention and explain your discomfort.
2. Examine the text books at your local school and\or your children's books for historical accuracy and anti-Jewish bias. If you find any inaccuracies, biases or omissions call this information to the attention of your school district and\or library. Talk to someone from the Anti-Defamation League of B'nai Brith and the Community Relations Committee of your local Jewish federation to see what else can be done. Discuss with your child what you found in the book(s) and what you did about it.
3. With other members of the group, act out a personal incident of antisemitism and try out different responses.

4. During the coming week watch the news for references to Jews and\or the State of Israel. List some words that are used to describe these Jews and\or Israel. Do you think that they were portrayed fairly or was the newscast biased? If you think the newscast is biased, write to the station to express your concerns.

5. *The Protocols of the Elders of Zion,* and materials published by The Institute for Historical Review, The Liberty Lobby, and The Committee for Open Debate on the Holocaust are among the most virulently antisemitic materials available. Make this known when you see it in your area, to the Anti-Defamation League of B'nai Brith and\or the Community Relations Committee of your local Jewish federation.

6. Organize a program for your organization to bring Jewish women together with women from other minority groups to discuss your shared concerns about racism, sexism, antisemitism.

7. The next time you hear a joke or remark which is antisemitic, racist or sexist, let the speaker know that you are offended.

# 3

# Israel and Zionism

## Changing perspectives: private and public

*Opening exercise: Can you remember an early childhood awareness of Israel? What were the circumstances? Who were the people connected to this memory? What is the feeling connected to this memory?*

1. During your childhood, what was expressed in your family about Israel and/or Zionism? Do you remember if any family members were involved in activities supporting or opposing Israel and/or Zionism? e.g. belonged to organizations such as Hadassah, ORT, Labor Zionists, American Council for Judaism, etc., raised funds, kept a Blue Box for Jewish National Fund, were involved with the Haganah, etc. What did they do?

2. When you were young were you involved in any such activities? How? e.g. going to a Zionist camp, visiting Israel, living on a kibbutz, belonging to Habonim, Young Judea, etc. What was the meaning of Israel and/or Zionism to you then?

3. Are you connected with Israel in any of the following ways: Reading articles and books about Israel? Following news about Israel in the press, radio and television? Subscribing to Israeli or Zionist publications? Attending lectures and educational programs? Studying Hebrew? Attending Israeli cultural activities? Contributing money

to support Israel? Raising money? Belonging to an organization whose purpose is to support Israel? Other? What is the meaning of Israel and/or Zionism for you now?

4. Have you ever been to Israel? If so, did you go with family, peers, Federation or organization tour, study program, ulpan, etc.? How did you feel when you first arrived? What did you see or experience that matched your expectations? That did not match? Did your trip(s) change how you felt about Israel? In what way? If you have not been to Israel would you like to go? If not, why not?

5. Do you have any family in Israel? Who are they? Are you in contact with them? Have you ever considered moving there? What would appeal to you about living there? What would have to change to make this more of a reality?

6. The United Jewish Appeal uses the phrase "We are One". Do you feel that Jews living outside of Israel (in diaspora) have a responsibility for Jews who live in Israel? Do you feel that *you* have such a responsibility? What form do you think it should take? Do you feel that Jews living in Israel have a responsibility for Jews living in the diaspora? What form do you think it should take?

7. Do you feel your government has a responsibility to support Israel financially? To sell arms to Israel? To act as a negotiator between the Arab states and Israel? Between the Palestinians and Israelis? How do you feel when your government takes a position about Israel that you strongly disagree with? How do you feel when the government of Israel takes a position that you strongly disagree with? Have *you* ever taken any action? e.g. written a letter to the newspaper, your legislator, contacted the Israeli consulate, participated in a demonstration or group activity, etc.

8. With whom are you comfortable discussing your opinions and feelings about Israel—family, Jewish friends, non-Jewish friends, classmates or teachers, etc.? Do you think that Jews should\should not criticize the policies and actions of the Israeli government? Do you think Jews who are critical of these policies and actions should refrain from

stating their opinions to other Jews? To mixed groups? To non-Jews? To the press and media?

9. How do you feel about the image of Israel in the media? How do you feel when you see pictures of Arabs attacking Israelis? When you see pictures of Israelis attacking Arabs? When you see pictures of Israelis and Arabs together in peaceful demonstrations? When you see pictures of Arab and Israeli women meeting together for peace?

10. When you were growing up what was your image of Israeli women? Has this changed for you? How?

11. Which of the following facts about women in Israel are familiar to you?

—A woman cannot obtain a divorce without the consent of her husband under any circumstances, even if her husband is physically violent or sexually abusive to her or their children.
—A childless woman whose husband dies is required by Jewish law to marry his brother unless the brother releases her from this obligation.
—A woman whose husband disappears or is missing-in-action is called an *agunah*. She is not allowed to remarry under rabbinic law.
—At the Western Wall in Jerusalem, women are forbidden to read from Torah scrolls, to chant or sing prayers aloud.
—At the time of this writing, women are 51% of the population of Israel and yet they are only 7% of members of Knesset. In the cabinet of 33 ministers none is a woman.*
—Women earn 70 shekels for every 100 shekels a man earns. Women make up 70% of the employees in the two lowest ranks of civil service, and only 3% of the top two ranks.*
—As rates of rape and violence against women increase, the existing shelters for battered women are desperately short of space and inadequately funded.

e.g. in a single month in 1991, 48 women applied to the shelter in Herzliya, but only 7 could be admitted.*

What is your response to this list? Does it raise issues you would like to know more about? Which? Are there any other issues of women's status in Israel that concern you? Have you personally taken action on these issues? How?

12. Do you feel women have something special to contribute to a peacemaking process? What is it? How can we begin?

*Closing exercise: Jewish events traditionally conclude with a prayer for peace (Oseh Shalom). Instead of this prayer we will go around and tell in one or two sentences our personal hope(s) for peace for Israel.*

## ACTIVITIES

1. Cut out news photos of Arabs and Jews in Israel from current newspapers and magazines. Use these pictures as a way to begin a discussion with friends and family about Israel.

2. Read the sections on Israel in *Deborah, Golda and Me* by Letty Cottin Pogreben (N.Y.: Crown Publishers, Inc., 1991, Chapters 15 and 16) and in *Chutzpah* by Alan M. Dershowitz (Boston: Little, Brown and Co., 1991, Chapter 7). Compare these points of view about Israel and the Palestinians.

3. Compare a news account in your local press about Israel with a description of the same event in the Jewish or Israeli press, or in a Zionist periodical. e.g. *Jerusalem Post, Hadassah Magazine,* your local Jewish Federation paper. (These should be available in a local synagogue library or Jewish Federation office) How are they the same? How are they different?

4. Contact local Jewish organizations to find out what they are doing to promote women's rights in Israel. Consider joining or giving financial support to the organization(s) doing the work you believe in.

5. Contact local peace groups (Jewish and\or non-Jewish) to find out

*Statistics from *Networking for Women,* Volume 4, Number 4, Israel Women's Network.

what they are doing to promote the peacemaking process in Israel. Consider joining or giving financial support to those you approve.

6. Find out if there are any ongoing dialogues between Jews and Arabs in your community and attend a session if that is possible. (To locate such a group, call your local Hillel group, American Jewish Congress, Israeli consulate, New Jewish Agenda).

7. Take it upon yourself to have your organization or school sponsor a program to educate people about women's rights in Israel.

# 4

# Into Action: Voting, Organizing, Creating Change

How we can impact the system through political action

*Opening exercise: Can you remember a time when you were part of a group working together toward a common goal? What was the group? What was the goal? What was satisfying about this experience to you?*

1. Are you a registered voter? When was the last time you voted? What kind of election? e.g. local, state\province, national. Have you ever voted for a winning candidate? For a woman—for what office? Have you ever chosen not to vote? e.g. didn't understand the ballot propositions, didn't like any of the candidates, felt like your vote didn't count, etc.

2. Can you think of an issue or problem in your school or local community that was changed by political action? What was it? Were you personally involved? How? (Some examples might be: pressured campus officials to create a program to educate male students about date rape, stopped the Board of Education from closing a neighborhood school, convinced the city council not to approve a high rise building in a residential community, got the municipal government to finance a senior center, etc.)

3. In your personal life what individual political actions do

you take? e.g. recycle paper, glass and aluminum, don't use certain cosmetics that are tested on animals, refuse to buy products whose ads degrade women, don't watch television programs or films which degrade women, don't buy war toys for children, don't eat veal, etc. What political actions do you take as part of a group? e.g. letter writing campaign, organized boycott of a store or product, sit-in, picket or teach-in at your school, phone calls to get out the vote for a particular candidate or proposition, etc.

4. Think about what issues are important to you now and of those select the one that is really the most important to you personally. What is it? Regarding this issue, which of the following actions have *you* taken as an individual?

Watched a television program, read a book or article
Discussed the issue with family or friends
Signed a petition
Circulated a petition
Voted for a candidate or ballot proposition
Attended a lecture or educational program
Attended a rally or demonstration
Attended a fund-raising activity
Attended a meeting
Asked a question or made a statement at a meeting
Participated in a panel or in a discussion group
Made phone calls to get others to participate
Wrote a letter to a corporation, legislator or
   government agency
Wrote a letter to the editor of a newspaper or magazine
Made a presentation to a group
Organized a group to take a stand on this issue
   (advocacy group)
Attended a class
Did research
Taught a class
Wrote an article, essay or book
Organized a public event
Testified at a government hearing

Participated in an act of civil disobedience
Was interviewed by the media
Donated money
Raised money
Other

Which of the things that you did was most satisfying to you? Why? Which was the hardest/ Why? Was there something you did that you didn't think you could do? What was it? Did you have any difficulties doing these actions because you were a woman? Because you were a Jew?

5. Regarding this issue or other issues that are important to you have you ever found yourself in any of the following situations?

Choosing not to voice an opinion to family, friends, partner\spouse
Choosing not to say what you think about this issue in writing to family, friends, etc.
Having strong opinions but choosing not to write that letter to the editor, legislator or corporation
Not responding to phone calls or letters about this issue
Not attending a meeting
Attending a meeting but not voicing your opinion or asking a question
Not signing a petition for a cause or candidate whom you support
Not joining a group which is doing something about this issue

Can you remember what it was that stopped you from expressing yourself? e.g. didn't feel your opinion mattered, didn't want to upset someone, didn't want to call attention to yourself, didn't want to get too involved, didn't know how to put your feelings into words, etc. How do you feel about these choices now?

6. Are you a member of a group or organization which takes\has taken action on this same issue? What is the organization? Regarding this group or organization: Who belongs to it? Women only? Women and men? Jews only? Jews and non-Jews? Caucasian only? Racially mixed? Single people? Married people? Heterosexuals? Lesbians and\ or gays? Bisexuals? the disabled? What is the purpose of this group? Is this group part of a national or international organization or is it an independent local group? Does your group work alone? Work with other groups in coalition for political action? What has your group been able to accomplish in regard to the issue you selected in question 4? Did the group do this alone or in coalition? Is the group planning any further actions regarding this issue? What are they? Will they be working alone or in coalition?

7. In support of your issue, which of the following actions have you taken as a member of this group?

> Volunteered to do a particular task e.g. take tickets, serve refreshments, help with mailing
> Served on a committee
> Chaired a committee
> Chaired an event
> Held an appointed office
> Held an elected office
> Represent your organization:
>> at a city council meeting
>> at a government hearing
>> in a coalition
>> at a local or national convention
> Lobbied legislators
> Wrote a grant proposal
> Organized a letter-writing campaign, demonstration or boycott
> Other

Which of these was most exciting and\or satisfying to you? Why? Which was the hardest? Why? Was there something you did that you didn't think you could do? What was it? Did you have any difficulty in this group because you are a woman? Because you are a Jew?

*Closing exercise: In our lives the actions we take are small steps which can provide us with hope that our world can be better. What is the one small step that you feel ready to take that you haven't taken before?*

## ACTIVITIES

Listed below are some current issues which are of concern to us as Jewish women:

Equal pay for women (comparable worth)

Equal social security &\or pension benefits for women

Discrimination in the work place based on age, sex, race, religion, disability and sexual orientation

Legal rights for unmarried couples (heterosexual or lesbian)

Availability of health insurance for all women

Programs and shelters for homeless women and children

Availability of affordable housing

Legal procedures to insure women's alimony and child support payments

Legal protection for women and children who are battered and\or sexually abused

Affirmative action for women and other minorities

Rise of acquaintance rape and date rape on campus

Rise of antisemitism expressed by other ethnic or racial minorities on campus

Legislation restricting availability and options for birth control and\or abortion

Availability of health care screening tests for all women (PAP smears, mammograms, blood tests for Tay-Sachs and other genetic diseases, etc.)

Inclusion of women as one-half of research population in all health studies (heart disease, lung cancer, etc.)

Increase amount of medical research on problems specific to women (breast and ovarian cancer, endometriosis, osteoporosis, etc.)

Availability of prenatal education and care for all women

Availability of programs and treatment for women and children with AIDS

Availability of health insurance to cover the choice of at-home or nursing home care

Access to transportation, housing and public places for women with disabilities

Access to equal credit rights for women

Race relations between women

Women's studies and Jewish studies on campus
The *agunah* and divorce laws in the Jewish community
Peace in the Middle East
Nuclear disarmament
Other (Add other issues which are important to you)

Looking at the above list, choose one issue which you would like to help change.

1. Read newspapers, magazines and other periodicals for a month. Gather any articles concerned with the issues you selected to be informed; find out who is involved, what different opinions are expressed, what organizations are taking a stand, what are the obstacles to change, and what is the current legal status. Find out at what level of government decisions are being made, and at what level of government current laws are being enforced.
2. Write a letter to someone who supports your position offering them support and encouragement. Write a letter to someone who opposes your position explaining why you disagree with them.
3. If you are not a registered voter, register to vote.
4. Write, call or visit your local government representative (city council member, county commissioner, student body representative, etc.) and find out how this issue is being addressed in your community or school by the government, discover what agencies and organizations are involved, and what she\he thinks the government's role is in addressing this issue. Voice your concerns to this person.
5. Contact your local agencies or organizations which are addressing this issue. Attend a few meetings or programs and listen to the opinions expressed. Talk informally with others who share your opinions. Consider which of these agencies or organizations you think you can work with and volunteer to help.
6. If you don't want to work with one of the existing organizations, or if there are none, find two or three other people who are also interested and share your concerns. Plan a small informational meeting to which you each invite a few friends. At this meeting gather the names of those who are interested in *doing* something about this issue.
7. Bring together those people who are interested in some action. At this meeting decide what it is you want to do as a group. Set some goals, and plan the first steps. (Refer to the section in the introduction, *Making a Group Decision.*
8. If the agenda of your group is to take political action, consider the following:

What is the lowest level of government (committee, sub-committee, commission, task force, etc) at which this issue is being discussed? Attend these meetings.
Who seem to be the key people at these meetings? Introduce yourself, your organization and make your concerns known to them.
If this issue if not being discussed or acted upon, find out how to get it on the agenda and do so.

Which legislators have shown concern for this or similar issues? Contact them to introduce yourself and your organization and urge them to introduce legislation.

Which other organizations are working on this or similar issues? Contact them to introduce your organization and explore the possibility of forming a coalition.

9. Encourage another woman in your group to develop her abilities. Support her in taking on new responsibilities and share with her the organizational and leadership skills which you have already acquired. Become her mentor.

# 5

# From Chance to Choice

How we feel about the future; our new choices
and our new roles


1. When you read or hear the words "man" or "mankind"
referring to all people, as in "One small step for man, one
giant leap for mankind," or "All men are created equal,"
how do you feel? Do you feel this language includes you?

What word would *you* choose to refer to all people?

2. Does it matter to you that words such as businessmen,
clergymen, and congressmen, etc. are assumed to include
the women in these professions?

What changes would you make in the language to reflect
the inclusion of women? e.g. chairperson instead of chair-
man, police officer instead of police man, congressional
representative instead of congressman, etc.

3. Does it matter to you that certain words set women ap-
art, such as poetess, Jewess, actress, housewife, coed, etc.

What changes would you make in the language to reflect
the equal status of women? e.g. poet, homemaker, student,
etc.

4. All men are addressed as "Mr." regardless of their marital status. Does it matter to you that women are addressed
as "Miss" or "Mrs." based on their marital status? How do
you feel about the use of "Ms"? How do you feel about a

woman taking her husband's name at marriage? Keeping her own name? Using both her name and her husband's name? How do you choose to be addressed at this time?

5. What does the word "sisterhood" mean to you as a Jewish woman? What appeals to you about the idea of sisterhood? e.g. trust, friendship, support, etc. What do you find difficult about this idea? If you wanted to make "sisterhood" more of a reality in your life, what would have to change?

6. What is your response when you read or hear the word "feminist"? What does this word mean to you? Here are some current feminist goals:

—Equal pay for equal work
—Equal social security &\ or pension benefits for women
—Ending discrimination in the workplace based on age, sex, race, religion, disability and sexual orientation
—Ending violence against women and children
—Changing behavior and attitudes toward rape and sexual harassment
—Preserving women's choice about when and whether to have children
—Availability of health care for all women
—Availability of prenatal education and care for all women
—Equal credit rights for women
—Equal representation of women in government
—Achieving peace in the world

Do you agree with most of these goals but are uncomfortable calling yourself a feminist? Why is that?
What would have to change for you to be comfortable calling yourself a feminist?

7. What is your response when you read or hear the phrase "traditional women's roles"? What would you say are the "traditional" roles that women are expected to fulfill? What appeals to you about these roles? What is not appealing?

Which of these have you done? Have you made any changes from "traditional" women's roles? What are they? Are there any changes you would like to make now or in the future? What are they?

8. In addition to the "traditional" roles women have been expected to fulfill, certain qualities of women have been romanticized and idealized. e.g. nurturing, listening, empathizing, maintaining relationships, protecting, keeping peace, etc. What do you value about these qualities? What do you find difficult? How do women use these special qualities at home? At work? In the community? Do you feel women have something special to contribute to politics? To government? To improving society? To making peace in the world?

9. Are the men in your family "traditional" with regard to women's roles? e.g. household chores, managing money, child care, etc. Are you able to discuss women's issues (as in Question 6) with the men in your family? How do these conversations make you feel? If you can't have such discussions, why not? What changes would you like to see the men in your family make, if any?

10. Are you able to discuss women's issues (as in Question 6) with the men outside your family, such as teachers, your rabbi, your boss or supervisor, etc.? How do these conversations make you feel? If you can't have such discussions, why not? Are these men "traditional" with regard to their opinions about sexual harassment, equal opportunity for advancement, child care, etc.? What changes would you like to see, if any?

11. How important is it to you that your partner be Jewish? How important is it to you that your children be Jewish? Your grandchildren? Do you feel that you have a responsibility as a Jewish woman to transmit Jewish customs, values and traditions to others? Who would you like to share these with? Who passed these values on to you? What have you been able to do to transmit Jewish values and traditions? What would you like to do?

12. As a Jewish woman do you feel that you have a responsibility to connect with Jewish women from other countries and cultures? From other economic groups? From other Jewish movements? What have you been able to do? What would you like to do? As a Jewish woman do you feel that you have a responsibility to connect with women from other ethnic groups? e.g. African-Americans, Latinas, Asians, Native Americans, etc. What have you been able to do? What would you like to do? Do you feel women have something special to contribute toward creating a society that respects our similarities and differences? What do you think that contribution could be?

*Closing exercise: We have become aware, as we have explored the journeys of our lives, that our choices, even those that don't appear important, have consequences for us and those around us: our choice to marry or not, to have children or not, who will be our life partner, what kind of work we will do, the education or training we get, where we volunteer our time and our service, where we donate our money, the political party we join or support, where we send our children to school, and more . . .*

*All of our choices make a difference, not only to us but to future generations and to the world in which we live. Can you think of an action that you can take that would be "One small step for a woman," and part of "A giant leap for woman-kind"?*

# RECOMMENDED READING

Background Books:

Baum, Charlotte, Hyman, Paula and Michel, Sonya. *The Jewish Woman in America.* NY: Dial, 1976; pap. Plume, NAL.

Belanky, M., Clinchy, B. Goldberger, N., Tarule, J., *Women's Ways of Knowing,* US:Basic Books, Inc., 1986.

Boston Women's Health Book Collective, *The New Our Bodies, Ourselves,* NY:Simon and Schuster, Inc. 1984

Cantor, Aviva. *The Jewish Woman: 1900–1985, Bibliography.* NY: Biblio Press, 1986.

Cott, Nancy F. *The Grounding of Modern Feminism.* New Haven: Yale Univ. Press, 1987.

Heschel, Susannah, ed., *On Being a Jewish Feminist: A Reader.* NY: Shocken, 1983.

Lerner, Anne Lapidus. "Who Hast Not Made Me A Man." The Movement for Equal Rights for Women in American Jewry. NY: American Jewish Committee, 1977. (pamphlet)

Marcus, Jacob Rader. *The American Jewish Woman: 1654–1980.* NY: Ktav, 1981.

Pogrebin, Letty Cottin. *Deborah, Golda and Me: Being Female and Jewish in America.* NY: Crown Publishers, 1991.

Schneider, Susan Weidman. *Jewish and Female: Choices & Changes in Our Lives Today.* NY: Simon & Schuster. 1984.

Shreve, Anita. *Women Together: Women Alone: The Legacy of the Consciousness Raising Movement.* NY: Fawcett. 1991.

Siegel, R. J., & Cole, E. *Seen But Not Heard, Jewish Women in Therapy.* N.Y. Harrington Park Press, 1990.

Taitz, E. and Henry S., *Written Out of History: Our Jewish Foremothers.* NY: Biblio Press, 1990 ed, pap. & cloth.

Umansky, Ellen. *Four Centuries of Jewish Women's Spirituality: A Source Book.* Boston, Ma.: Beacon Press, forthcoming 1992.

*Working It Out* (23 women contributors on their feminist experiences) NY: Pantheon, 1977.

For the following, please refer to CONTENTS at front of book and topics listed:

I. 2.
"Jewish Families Are Different," focus issue, *LILITH,* Spring, 1989.

I. 3

Tavris, Carol. "My Mother, the Feminist," *LILITH,* Summer, 1989, pp. 10–11.

I. 7

Laws, Sophie. *Issues of Blood: the Politics of Menstruation.* Irvington, N.Y.: New York University Press, 1990.

I. 8.

Balka, Christie & Rose, Andy. *Twice Blessed: On Being Lesbian, Gay and Jewish.* Boston: Beacon Press, 1989.

Goldberg, Herb. *The New Male Female Relationship.* NY: Morrow & Co. 1983.

"Single and Jewish: Communal Perspectives" NY: *American Jewish Committee,* pamphlet.

Gold, Michael, "God in the Bedroom," *Moment Magazine,* August, 1991, p. 36.

Brewer, J. S., Davidman, L. and Avery E., *Sex and the Modern Jewish Woman,* Bibliography/Guide. NY: Biblio Press, 1986.

I. 9.

Ehrensaft, Diane. *Parenting Together: Men and Women Sharing the Care of Their Children.* NY: The Free Press, 1987.

Cantor, Carla. "Coming Out in the Jewish Family," *LILITH,* Summer, 1989, pp. 23–25.

Hyman, Paula. "The Jewish Family: Looking for a Usable Past," S. Heschel, *Op. Cit.,* pp. 19–26.

Rubin, Lillian B., *Women of a Certain Age: The Midlife Search for Self.* NY: Harper & Row, 1979.

Scarf, Mimi. "Marriages Made in Heaven? Battered Jewish Wives," in S. Heschel, *Op. Cit.,* pp. 51–64.

Spiegel, Marcia Cohn. *The Last Taboo: Dare We Speak About Incest.* Lilith, Summer 1988, pp. 10–12.

II. 1.

Bletter, D. and Grinker, L., *The Invisible Thread.* (Photos and interviews of American Jewish women) Phila. Pa.: Jewish Publication Society, 1990.

Fishman, Sylvia. "The Impact of Feminism on American Jewish Life," *American Jewish Yearbook,* 1989, pp. 3–62. NY: American Jewish Committee.

Freedman, Estelle B., "Small Group Pedagogy: Consciousness Raising in Conservative Times," *NWSA Journal,* v. 2, No. 4, Fall, 1990.

II. 2.

Hertzberg, Arthur. "Gender," *Judaism,* rev. ed. 1991, pp. 115–130, NY: Simon & Schuster

Lackow, M. P., "In the Russian Gymnasia," *LILITH,* Winter, 1990, pp. 15–20.

II. 3.

Kent, D., "Offense Intended: JAP-Bashing on College Campuses," *Seventeen.* April, 1990, p. 90ff.

II. 4.

Biale, Rachel. *Women and Jewish Law.* NY: Schocken Books, 1984.

Marder, Janet. "How Women Are Changing the Rabbinate," *Reform Judaism,* Summer, 1991, p. 4-ff.

II. 5.

Bergmann, Barbara R. *The Economic Emergence of Women.* NY: Basic Books, 1987.

Remick, Helen, ed. *Comparable Worth and Wage Discrimination.* Phila. Pa.: Temple University Press, 1984.

II. 7.

Gutek, Barbara A. *Sex in the Workplace.* San Francisco: Jossey-Bass, 1985.

Henning, M. and Jardim, A., *The Managerial Woman.* NY: Anchor Press, 1976.

II. 8.

Erens, Patricia. *The Jew in American Cinema.* Bloomington, IN: Indiana University Press, 1984.

II. 9.

Adelman, Penina V. *Miriam's Well:* Rituals for Jewish Women Around the Year. NY: Biblio Press, 1990 ed.

Broner, E. M. *A Weave of Women.* NY: Holt, 1978. Indiana Univ. Pr., 1985.

Eilberg, Amy. "Encountering a Feminine God," *MOMENT,* April, 1989. pp. 34–38.

Kass, L., Rebecca: A Woman for All Seasons. *Commentary,* Sept. 1991. pp. 30–5.

Plaskow, Judith. *Standing Again At Sinai:* Judaism from a Feminist Perspective. San Francisco: Harper/Collins, 1990.

III. 1.

Dworkin, A., *Mercy.* NY: Four Walls Eight Windows, 1991.

Orbach, Susie. *Fat is a Feminist Issue.* Vols. I and II, 1978 & 1982, Berkley & Hamlyn, London.

Schwartz, Hillel. *Never Satisfied: A Cultural History of Diets, Fantasies and Fat.* NY: Free Press/Macmillan, 1986.

III. 2.

Beck, Evelyn Torton. "The Politics of Jewish Invisibility," *NWSA Journal,* v. 1, no. 1, 1988. pp. 93–102.

Eber, L., Kaye/Kantrowitz, M. and Klepfisz, I. *Awareness and Action: A Source Book on Antisemitism.* NY: New Jewish Agenda, 1991.

Glenn, Susan A., *Daughters of the Shtetl: Life and Labor in the Immigrant Generation.* Ithaca: Cornell Univ. Press, 1991.

Pogrebin, Letty Cottin, "Antisemitism in the Women's Movement," *MS Magazine,* June 1982.

Weinberg, Sidney Stahl. *World of Our Mothers.* University of N.C. Press, 1988.

"Face to Face: Black-Jewish Campus Dialogues," NY: American Jewish Committee. (pamphlet)

III.3.

Dworkin, A., "Israel: Whose Country Is it?" *MS Magazine,* Sept./Oct. 1990, pp. 68–79.

Falbel, Rita; Klepfisz, Irena and Nevel, Donna. *Jewish Women's Call for Peace.* Ithaca: Firebrand Books, 1990.

Swirski, B. and Safir, M. P., *Calling the Equality Bluff: Women in Israel.* Pergamon/Teachers College Press, 1991.

III. 4.

Garland, Anne Witte. *Women Activists: Challenging the Abuse of Power.* NY: The Feminist Press, 1989.

Welch, S. and Ullrich, F., *The Political Life of American Jewish Women.* NY: Biblio Press, 1984.

III. 5.

Bershtel, Sara and Graubard, Allen. *Saving Remnants: Feeling Jewish in America.* NY: Macmillan, 1991.

Hauptman, Hyman and Umansky, "American Feminism and Jewish Women," *Jews in America: Dreams and Realities,* by N. Cohen and R. M. Seltzer. NY: New York University Press. (forthcoming 1993)

Miller, Casey & Swift, Kate, *The Handbook of Nonsexist Writing.* NY: Harper & Row, 2nd ed., 1988.

Maggio, Rosalie, *The Nonsexist Word Finder.* Boston: Beacon Press, 1990.

# RESOURCES:

See American Jewish Yearbook (in your local synagogue library) for a complete list of Jewish periodicals.

Consult Tsena Rena section of LILITH Magazine, HADASSAH Magazine, *The Council Woman, Na'amat Woman, Women's American ORT Reporter,* and other house organs of Jewish women's groups for further information, also: *Bridges, "A Journal for Jewish Feminists and Our Friends",* P.O. Box 18437, Seattle WA 98118. *Lilith: Jewish Women's Magazine,* 250 West 57th St., NY, NY 10019, *MS,* 230 Park Ave., NY, NY 10169.

See *Index to Jewish Periodicals* in your Judaica library for articles on specific topics.

Additional information:

Jewish Working Group on Domestic Violence
Jewish Family & Children's Service
1610 Spruce St.
Philadelphia, Pa. 19107

STAAR: Students Together Against Acquaintance Rape (Student sponsored educational group)
%Office of Health Education
Student Health Service
Box 745 HUP
Philadelphia, Pa. 19104-4283
215 662-7126

For a newsletter about Israeli women issues:
Networking for Women, the Israel Women's Network, POB 3171, Jerusalem, (91031, Israel.

For information on "How To Start A Jewish Women's Book Collection" in your local synagogue library, JWB Jewish Book Council, 15 E. 26th St., New York, NY 10010. ($3.50)

The Jewish Women's Resource Center of the NYC National Council of Jewish Women has a list of publications on Jewish women rituals and other topics. Write: JWRC, NCJW, 9 E. 69th St., New York, NY 10021.